MW00984285

What Every Catholic Needs to Know About the Bible

A Parish Guide to Scripture

Kay Murdy

Resource Publications, Inc.
San Jose, California

Also in this series: *What Every Catholic Needs to Know about the Mass, What Every Catholic Needs to Know about Advent and Christmas, What Every Catholic Needs to Know about Lent, Triduum, and Easter*

© 2004 Resource Publications, Inc. All rights reserved. No part of this book may be photocopied or otherwise reproduced without permission from the publisher. For reprint permission, contact:

Reprint Department
Resource Publications, Inc.
160 E. Virginia Street #290
San Jose, CA 95112-5876
(408) 286-8505 voice
(408) 287-8748 fax

Library of Congress Cataloging-in-Publication Data
Murdy, Kay, 1936-
    What every Catholic needs to know about the Bible : a parish guide to Bible study /
       Kay Murdy
      p. cm.
    "A comprehensive and highly readable guide. All the necessary tools for studying and
    praying the Scriptures in a meaningful way for the contemporary Catholic."
    Includes bibliographical references (p.).
    ISBN 0-89390-604-2
      1. Bible—Study and teaching— Catholic Church. I. Title.

BS587.M87 2004
220'.088'282—dc22

                                             2003066731
Printed in the United States of America

Production Staff: Nelson Estarija, Elizabeth Gebelein, Susan Carter

New Revised Standard Version Bible, © 1989, Division of Christian Education of the National Council of the Churches of Christ in the United States of America. Used by permission. All rights reserved.

Excerpts from Dogmatic Constitution on Divine Revelation *Dei Verbum*, © 1965 Libreria Editrice Vaticana, 00120 Città del Vaticano. Used by permisson. All rights reserved.

Dedicated to the team members, faculty and students of the Catholic Bible Institute

Cosponsored by the Los Angeles Archdiocesan Office of Religious Education and the Center for Religion and Spirituality, Loyola Marymount University, Los Angeles, California

Contents

Introduction: Finding Your Way around the Bible 1

1
What Does the Catholic Church Teach about the Bible? 11

2
The Handing On of Divine Revelation 19

3
Sacred Scripture, Its Inspiration and Interpretation 23

4
Understanding the Old Testament. 31

5
Understanding the New Testament 47

6
Sacred Scripture in the Life of the Church. 63

Bibliography: Basic Tools for Bible Study 81

Acknowledgments

With gratitude to my friends and teachers whose expertise and thoughtful critiques assisted me in writing this book.

Rev. Felix Just, SJ, PhD
Director, Center for Religion and Spirituality
Loyola Marymount University, Los Angeles, California

Rev. J. Patrick Mullen, PhD, STL
Assistant Professor, Biblical Studies
St. John's Seminary, Camarillo, California

Mary Ann Getty-Sullivan, PhD, STL, STD
Associate Professor, Sacred Scripture
Saint Vincent College, Latrobe, Pennsylvania

Rev. Thomas Welbers
Pastor, Our Lady of the Assumption Parish, Claremont, California

"Your word is a lamp to my feet and a light to my path"
(Ps 119:105).

Introduction: Finding Your Way around the Bible

J esus tells us, "I am the way, and the truth, and the life" (Jn 14:6).[1] Sometimes, it is a difficult task to find our way in the Bible in our search for truth and life. Non-Catholic perspectives may also confuse us. Catholics need to study the Bible in a manner faithful to our own spiritual tradition. So let's begin by asking, "What do Catholics need to know about the Bible?"

What does the word "Bible" mean?

The Greek word *biblios*, for "Bible," translated into Latin, *biblia*, means "book." For Christians and Jews, the Bible is "The Book." But the Bible is more than a single book; it is a collection of books, a small library. As in any library, you will find a variety of books—prose, poetry, history, and so on. In the Bible we find two large groups of books:

- The Old Testament — The Hebrew Scriptures
- The New Testament — The Christian Scriptures

The word "old" does not mean that the Old Testament is outmoded and no longer useful. For Christians, it simply means the Jewish Bible or the Hebrew Scriptures. For both Jews and Christians, the Bible is a testimony to the God whom they worship.

What does the word "testament" mean?

When you hear the word "testament" you might think of "last will and testament." The word "testament" is from the Latin word *testamentum* that translates the Hebrew word *berît*, both of which mean "covenant," a pact or agreement that God made with people.

> If you obey my voice and keep my covenant, you shall be my treasured possession out of all the peoples (Ex 19:5).

For Christians, the covenant is fulfilled in the New Covenant in Jesus Christ. God did not revoke the covenant with the Jewish people; it is irrevocable and unconditional.

How are the books of the Old Testament divided?

The books of the Old Testament, written in Hebrew and Aramaic, are arranged, numbered, and titled in several different ways in Jewish, Orthodox, Catholic, or Protestant Bibles. Ancient and modern Jews divide their Bible into three parts:

1. The five books of the Law (Hebrew, *Torah*, also called the *Pentateuch*, a Greek word meaning "five books") are: Genesis, Exodus, Leviticus, Numbers, and Deuteronomy.

2. The eight books of the Prophets (Hebrew, *Nevi'im*) are divided into two groups, the former prophets (that Christians call the "Historical Books"): Joshua, Judges, Samuel, and Kings; and the three latter prophets: Isaiah, Jeremiah, Ezekiel. The twelve minor prophets, considered as one book, are: Hosea, Joel, Amos,

Obadiah, Jonah, Micah, Nahum, Habakkuk, Zephaniah, Haggai, Zechariah, and Malachi.

3. The eleven books of the Writings (Hebrew, *Ketuvim*, also called the *Hagiographa*, a Greek word meaning "holy writings") are: Psalms, Proverbs, Job, Song of Songs, Ruth, Lamentations, Ecclesiastes (Qoheleth), Esther, Daniel, Ezra-Nehemiah, and 1 and 2 Chronicles.[2]

By taking the first letter of each of these Hebrew titles—*Torah, Nevi'im, Ketuvim*—the acronym *Tanakh* was formed, the word for Judaism's sacred Scriptures.[3] Most Christian Bibles have adopted the ancient Greek order of the Jewish Scriptures, which arranges the books of the Old Testament in four parts:

1. The Pentateuch

2. The historical books[4]

3. The wisdom books

4. The prophetic books

The placement of the prophetic books has an impact on how Jews and Christians understand the Old Testament. For Jews, the prophets were the interpreters of the Torah and they belonged with the first five books. For Christians, the prophets anticipated the Messiah and were placed at the end of the Old Testament, right before the Gospels.

How many books are in the Old Testament?

The number of books in the Old Testament depends on which version you are using. There are twenty-four books in the Hebrew Bible,[5] thirty-nine in the Protestant, and forty-six in the Catholic, and even more in Orthodox Bibles. You probably are wondering, "What are these extra seven books in the Catholic Bible?"

For the answer we need to go back to the conquest of Alexander the Great (336–323 BCE[6]). After Alexander conquered the world from Greece to Persia and as far as India in the East, his native Greek tongue became the dominant language. Greek-speaking Jews who lived outside the land of Israel needed a translation of the Bible they could understand.[7] The legend is that, in the third century before the time of Christ, seventy Jewish scholars were commissioned to translate the Hebrew Bible into Greek in Alexandria, Egypt. Supposedly they worked independently and arrived at the same translation in seventy days.[8] This translation is called the "Septuagint" (Latin for "70," abbreviated LXX). It included seven books that were either written in Greek or at a later date.[9] These books are Tobit, Judith, 1 and 2 Maccabees, Wisdom, Sirach (also called Ecclesiasticus), and Baruch, as well as later additions to Daniel and Esther. Catholics and Orthodox Christians call these seven books *deuterocanonical*, meaning "second canon," not because they are less important but because they were settled at a later time than the *protocanonical* books, or the "first canon."

What is meant by the "canon" of the Bible?

A "canon," meaning "rule" or "standard," is a collection of texts considered authoritative and divinely inspired and therefore included in the Bible. At the time of Jesus there was no agreement among Jews or Christians on what constituted the "Scriptures" (which means "writings"). Toward the end of the first century of the Christian era, some Jewish scholars met to determine the official list of the Scriptures. Certain books of the Old Testament, the Law and the Prophets along with many of the Writings, had already achieved an authoritative status within the Jewish community. Other writings were disputed and were rejected, including the extra seven books in the Greek Septuagint and later additions to the Hebrew text.

As Christianity spread from Israel throughout the ancient Mediterranean world, the majority of Christians spoke Greek. They used the Greek Septuagint translation of the Bible that their Greek-speaking Jewish neighbors used. When the books of the New Testament were written, the authors cited most Old Testament passages directly from the Septuagint.

By the year 110 CE, Christian writers were quoting the four Gospels—Matthew, Mark, Luke, and John. By the year 200 CE, the four Gospels, the Acts of the Apostles, and some letters written by Paul, Peter, and John were already regarded as sacred Scripture equal to the Hebrew Testament. St. Athanasius, Bishop of Alexandria, made the first known list of the twenty-seven books of the New Testament (all written in Greek) in 367 CE.

By the fourth century most Christians spoke Latin and no longer understood Greek. Around 382 CE, Pope Damasus wanted a single "authorized" Latin version of the Bible. He asked Jerome, a Latin scholar, to translate the Gospels, Psalms, and other books of the Old Testament into Latin from the original languages.

During the Protestant Reformation of the sixteenth century, Martin Luther translated the Bible from the original languages into German. The reformers restricted their Old Testament to the books of the Hebrew canon and rejected the additional books of the Septuagint, which they called "apocryphal" (meaning "hidden").[10] They also called into question the letters of James, 2 Peter, 2 and 3 John, and Jude, and the books of Hebrews and Revelation, although they later accepted them.

The Catholic reaction to the Protestant Reformation came with the Council of Trent (1545–63). The council fathers accepted the forty-six Old Testament books of the Septuagint, following what appeared to them as a firm tradition of the church from ancient times. St. Jerome's Latin Vulgate (meaning "common" or "popular") became the official translation of the Bible for Catholics for centuries. An English translation of the Latin Vulgate known as the Douay-Rheims Bible was later produced in France. The New Testament was published at Rheims (1582) and the Old Testament at Douai (1609–10). The King James Bible, authorized by James of England and published in 1611, became the most influential translation of the Bible in the English-speaking Protestant world for more than 300 years. The Revised Standard Version and New Revised Standard Version are successors to the King James Version.

In 1944, a group of Catholic scholars in the United States under the patronage of the Confraternity of Christian Doctrine produced a translation of the Bible in contemporary English from the original languages. Since that time, a better understanding of Hebrew and Greek and the development of textual criticism continue to make more accurate translations of the sacred text possible.

How many books are in the New Testament?

The New Testament list of 27 books is identical for all Christians, but it was not always so. During the first two centuries of Christianity, a variety of other Gospels, Acts, Epistles, and Apocalypses never made the "final cut." Such writings as the Gospel of Thomas were rejected early in the church's history. Marcion's heretical idea of dropping the Old Testament and de-Judaizing the New Testament was also rejected. On the other hand, the Didache (Greek, "teaching"), a handbook of moral behavior and church practice, seemed worthy of inclusion but was not placed in the final canon. Apparently, there were three criteria in determining the canonicity of a document:

1. *Apostolic origin* — A document that was clearly non-apostolic was rejected.

2. *The rule of faith* — A document must faithfully reflect the teaching of Jesus and the apostles.

3. *The consensus of the church* — A document must have been used and accepted by the early Christian churches.

It was not until the fourth century that the canon of the Bible was considered "closed." The Roman Catholic canon was fixed at the Council of Hippo in 393 CE and reaffirmed by the two Councils of Carthage in 397 and 419. In 1546 the Council of Trent officially ratified the canon of the New Testament.

Like the Old Testament, the New Testament is not a single book but a library of books:

- Four "Gospels" — Matthew, Mark, Luke, and John

- One "Acts" — The Acts of the Apostles[11]

- Twenty-one "letters" or "epistles" written by Paul and other authors

- One "Apocalypse" — The Book of Revelation[12]

How do we find our way around the Bible?

For centuries there were no chapters or verses in the Bible to help find a particular passage. In the thirteenth century, the books of the Bible were divided into chapters for the first time by Stephen Langton, a professor in Paris. In 1551 a Parisian book printer, Robert Estienne, is credited with dividing those chapters into verses (often arbitrary), supposedly while traveling on horseback from Paris. As the story goes, every time the horse bounced, that is where the printer placed his verse number. Thus we have our modern division of chapters and verses in the Christian Bible, which was later adopted by Jews for the Old Testament.

When did the Bible become a "book"?

Since the Bible was not originally a book but a collection of scrolls, finding a text was very difficult, especially if it occurred toward the middle or end of the roll. When Jesus was handed the scroll to read in a synagogue in Nazareth, he unrolled it and searched for the book of Isaiah (Lk 4:17).[13] It wasn't until the second century that the "codex," or "book" in our sense of the term, emerged. The codex not only made it easier to find the location of a particular text, it made it possible to put all the books of the Old and New Testaments in a single volume.

Until the advent of printing with movable type, the Bible wasn't available to the general public. One of the first books printed was the Gutenberg Bible, a Latin version, around 1456 CE. Before that, every copy of the Bible, called manuscripts, had to be meticulously copied by hand—letter by letter—in monasteries or universities. When a Bible was worn out, the copyists spent years making a fresh copy. Books were so valuable that when a Bible was placed in a church, it would often be chained to the reading desk to stop anyone from stealing it. For centuries, Christians had to rely on public proclamation and preaching for their understanding of the Bible. Except for the educated upper class, most people were unable to read or write. Even today, vast numbers of the world's population are illiterate. Private Bible study, such as you and I engage in, is a great privilege.

How do we find a particular passage in the Bible?

When searching for a text in the Bible, first locate the book, then turn to the chapter, and then search for the particular verse you want. The names of the books of the Bible are usually abbreviated in a reference. For instance, Genesis may be abbreviated "Gen" or "Gn," depending on your version of the Bible. The first number following the title of the book is the chapter—Genesis, chapter one, would be written "Gen 1." The next number or numbers indicate the verse or verses. One way to separate chapter from verse is by a comma (more common in Europe); another by a colon (usually in the United States). Genesis, chapter two, verse one, could be written thus: "Gen 2,1" or "Gen 2:1."

A hyphen or en dash is used to indicate several verses: Gen 3:14–16 indicates Genesis, chapter three, verses fourteen to sixteen. A hyphen or en dash can also signify several chapters: Gen 2–5 denotes Genesis, chapters two through five. A comma separates different verses in the same chapter. Gen 2:4,8,11 indicates Genesis, chapter two, verses four, eight, and eleven. If you want to indicate only a part of a verse, you add lower-case letters to the numbers. Thus Gen 2:4a indicates Genesis chapter two and the first part of verse four. Gen 2:4b would indicate Genesis chapter two and the last part of verse four. This may seem very complicated, but you will soon get the hang of it.

Endnotes

1. The New Revised Standard Version of the Bible is used throughout this work.

2. Ruth and Daniel are considered "writings" in the Hebrew Bible. In Christian Bibles, Ruth and Esther are considered "historical books" and Daniel is listed as one of the "prophets."

3. The word "Torah" refers to the first five books of the written Scriptures; however, Jews believe that in its broadest sense the entire Bible along with the oral Law is the Torah, instruction for Jewish life and faith.

4. The six historical books (Joshua, Judges, 1 and 2 Samuel, 1 and 2 Kings) are called "deuteronomic history." They form one narrative from the entry into the Promised Land to the fall of Jerusalem in 587 BCE. The last large group of books (1 and 2 Chronicles,

Ezra-Nehemiah) is called the "chronicler's history" because it begins with the Book of Chronicles.

5. The breaking of Samuel, Kings, Chronicles, Ezra and Nehemiah into two parts is an artifact of Christians who first issued these books that were too big to be published as single volumes. Because everyone followed these standards, the numbers 1 and 2 were attached to Samuel, Kings, and Chronicles, while Ezra and Nehemiah became two books. Jews count the twelve minor prophets as one book, while Christians count them as twelve separate books.

6. Traditionally, dates are written "BC" (Before Christ) and "AD" (Latin for *Anno Domini*, "in the year of the Lord"). These designations are specifically Christian. Out of respect for Jews, Muslims, and other religions, contemporary scholars often use the terms "BCE" (Before the Common Era) and "CE" (Common Era) as a means of dating historical events.

7. The "dispersion" of Jews throughout the world after the Babylonian Exile is called the *Diaspora*.

8. The number 7 in the Bible means "complete" or "perfect," a number rendered sacred by the seventh day, the Sabbath (Ex 20:11).

9. Portions of some of these texts written in Hebrew were found in the Dead Sea Scrolls at Qumran, suggesting that some of them were probably composed in Hebrew. Those texts were lost and, until now, the Greek translations were the only ones in existence.

10. Today, some Protestant editions of the Bible include the seven apocryphal (deutero canonical) books in their Bibles in an appendix or in a special section between the Old and New Testaments.

11. The Acts of the Apostles is not "historical" in the modern sense, such as a biography or a factual chronology of events. Like other biblical books, it is a faith record written by believers to inspire others to proclaim God's word.

12. The Book of Revelation actually contains three styles of writing: letter, prophetic, and apocalyptic.

13. The Book of Isaiah appears as a single book in our Bibles, but most scholars agree that it is three collections composed by the prophet Isaiah and his disciples. Book I, chapters 1–39, First Isaiah, is attributed to Isaiah of Jerusalem, who wrote in the eighth century before the Exile. Book II, chapters 40–55, Second Isaiah, is the writings of an anonymous author during the Exile. Book III, chapters 55–66, Third Isaiah, contains later oracles composed after the Exile.

What Does the Catholic Church Teach about the Bible?

Since the Second Vatican Ecumenical Council (1962–65) Catholics have had a growing interest in the Bible. Until then most Catholics didn't read the Bible on a regular basis. In 1943 Pope Pius XII issued his encyclical *Divino Afflante Spiritu*, which promoted Scripture study in the Catholic Church. Some twenty years later, the Vatican Council produced a remarkable document to guide Catholics in their understanding of Scripture, called the *Dogmatic Constitution on Divine Revelation* (*Dei Verbum*, Latin for "Word of God"). The document is entitled "dogmatic," which signifies that it contains authoritative truth necessary for the whole church. *Dei Verbum* is made up of six chapters and is printed in many Catholic editions of the Bible. Unfortunately, most of us have never read this important church document. Perhaps we are waiting for it to be made into a movie!

Dogmatic Constitution on Divine Revelation: Dei Verbum

Pope Paul VI solemnly promulgated the *Dogmatic Constitution on Divine Revelation* on November 18, 1965.

> Hearing the word of God with reverence and proclaiming it with faith, the sacred synod ... wishes to set forth authentic doctrine on divine revelation and how it is handed on, so that by hearing the message of salvation the whole world may believe, by believing it may hope, and by hoping it may love (DV 1).[1]

Dei Verbum begins with God's act of self-disclosure:

> In His goodness and wisdom God chose to reveal Himself and to make known to us the hidden purpose of His will (see Eph 1:9) by which through Christ, the Word made flesh, man might in the Holy Spirit have access to the Father and come to share in the divine nature (see Eph 2:18; 2 Peter 1:4) (DV 2).[2]

The entire Bible, Old and New Testament alike, is the product of people of faith, Jews and Christians, in their attempt to understand God's revelation to them. The word "revelation" (Greek, *apokalupsis*) means to "uncover" something that was concealed. Divine revelation is not merely a disclosure of facts and information formerly unknown to us. Through God's revelation in the Bible, we come to *know* God, not just *know about* God.

How does God speak to us?

Dei Verbum states that God gives "an enduring witness to Himself in created realities (see Rom. 1:19–20)" (DV 3). It can be said that all of creation is a visible sign revealing God's hidden presence. The psalmist cries out, "The heavens are telling the glory of God; and the firmament proclaims his handiwork" (Ps 19:1).

God's word is a creative energy, echoing throughout the limitless universe. God's voice is heard in the pounding ocean waves, in the roar of the lion, the hum of bees, and the songs of dolphins and birds. God speaks in human laughter and tears, in shouts of victory and sighs of defeat, in murmurs of love, in a baby's cry, and in the rattle of death. Sometimes God's words are like thunder (Sir 43:17) and, at times, a mere whisper (Job 4:12). Paul writes that even non-believers can know God through natural knowledge:

> Ever since the creation of the world his eternal power and divine nature, invisible though they are, have been understood and seen through the things he has made. So they are without excuse (Rom 1:20).

God's word is also known through the course of human events, called "salvation history." God's word heard at creation was the voice that led the people through the sea to freedom in the Promised Land. God's self-revelation also came to individuals, as *Dei Verbum* states:

> Planning to make known the way of heavenly salvation, He went further and from the start manifested Himself to our first parents. Then after their fall His promise of redemption aroused in them the hope of being saved (see Gen 3:15)(DV 3).

God's word led the people to the Promised Land and resounded on Mount Sinai, with ten commandments (Greek, *dekalogos*, "ten words") to Moses and the people, teaching them how to live in right relationship with God and one another. The Hebrew word *dabar* is the most common word for "speak." The prophets, God's intermediaries or "spokespersons," were called by God regardless of their limitations. Jeremiah revealed his own reluctance to speak God's words:

> If I say, "I will not mention him, or speak any more in his name," then within me there is something like a burning fire shut up in my bones; I am weary with holding it in, and I cannot (Jer 20:9).

The prophet Isaiah said that God's word had a power of its own:

> For as the rain and the snow come down from heaven, and do not return there until they have watered the earth, making it bring forth and sprout, giving seed to the sower and bread to the eater, so shall my word be that

goes out from my mouth; it shall not return to me empty, but it shall accomplish that which I purpose, and succeed in the thing for which I sent it (Isa 55:10–11).

For centuries, God's revelation was communicated orally through stories, histories, laws, customs, songs, and worship. Gradually, over a long period of time, involving hundreds of individuals, the Hebrew Scriptures were compiled so that they might be kept as a record for future generations (Isa 30:8). With joy God's people recorded their triumphs and victories and with humility they reported their sorrows and defeats, especially their failure to keep the covenant God gave them. The prophet Jeremiah expressed their yearning for a permanent relationship with God, not written on tablets of stone but carved on the hearts of the people (Jer 31:31-33). In his incarnation, Jesus Christ is God's revelation of the New Covenant, the "Word made flesh" (Jn 1:1–18), as *Dei Verbum* states:

> For He sent His Son, the eternal Word, who enlightens all men, so that He might dwell among men and tell them of the innermost being of God (see John 1:1–18) (DV 4).

Through Jesus' words and deeds, his signs and miracles, but especially by his death and resurrection, he revealed that God is with us to deliver us from sin and death and raise us up to life eternal. We can say that Jesus is the "last word" of God's revelation, and we await no further revelation. *Dei Verbum* teaches that public revelation (intended for the whole church) ended with the close of the New Testament era. No private revelations (such as personal visions or apparitions) add anything essential to the faith (DV 4).

At the same time, the process by which we try to understand God's word and apply it to our lives goes on through reflection and the teaching of the church. An example is the message of freedom Jesus proclaimed for all people: "So if the Son makes you free, you will be free indeed" (Jn 8:36). Later we hear, "Slaves, obey your earthly masters in everything" (Col 3:22). Slavery was an accepted institution and early Christians did not have the power to overcome it. In fact, slavery was not abolished in the United States until the Emancipation Proclamation in 1862. Through prayer and study the church must continually examine social structures and institutions that keep people in bondage.

How should we respond to God's word?

God speaks all the time—in the church and the sacraments, through other people and events, and especially in the sacred Scriptures. However, just as the prophets were spurned and ignored, so too God's voice is often disregarded. *Dei Verbum* states that although God initiates revelation, there must be a corresponding response from the receiver:

> "The obedience of faith" (Rom 13:26; see 1:5; 2 Cor 10:5–6) "is to be given to God who reveals, an obedience by which man commits his whole self freely to God, offering the full submission of intellect and will to God who reveals" (DV 5).[3]

When we read the Bible, an exchange occurs between the biblical text and ourselves; otherwise, it is just ink on paper and has no relevance to our lives. The author of Hebrews wrote that God's word is a life-giving, transforming power:

> Indeed, the word of God is living and active, sharper than any two-edged sword, piercing until it divides soul from spirit, joints from marrow; it is able to judge the thoughts and intentions of the heart (Heb 4:12).

St. Augustine, bishop and Doctor of the Church, understood this when he wrote his book *Confessions*.[4] During his misspent youth he prayed that God would change his heart—but not right away. One day, as he prayed in his garden, he probed the inner recesses of his soul. A great storm seemed to break within him, and he cried out, "How long, how long this 'tomorrow and tomorrow.' Why not now?" He then heard the voice of a young child chanting, "Take it and read it! Take it and read it!" Augustine reached for his Bible and read from Paul's Letter to the Romans as if the words were spoken directly to himself:

The night is far gone, the day is near. Let us then lay aside the works of darkness and put on the armor of light; let us live honorably as in the day, not in reveling and drunkenness, not in debauchery and licentiousness, not in quarreling and jealousy. Instead, put on the Lord Jesus Christ, and make no provision for the flesh, to gratify its desires (Rom 13:12–14).

Augustine was converted by the power of this passage. He returned to Christianity and was baptized in 376 CE, later becoming the bishop of Hippo in North Africa. Paul certainly didn't have Augustine in mind when he wrote his letter to the church in Rome. He was writing to people in his own particular time and circumstances. Our understanding of the Bible is also shaped by the social, cultural, religious, and personal context in which we live. By engaging in a conversation with the text, we are opened up to the larger world in which we live.

Throughout the centuries the Bible continues to be an instrument that touches and moves human hearts. Our hope in reading the Bible is that God will transform us and that this transformation will cause our church, our society, and our world to act with truth (Hebrew, *'emeth*), justice (Hebrew, *mishpat*), and righteousness (Hebrew, *tsedeq*). The first chapter of *Dei Verbum* ends by stressing God's desire to reveal eternal truth to us in ways we could not understand on our own:

Through divine revelation, God chose to show forth and communicate Himself and the eternal decisions of His will regarding the salvation of men. That is to say, He chose to share with them those divine treasures which totally transcend the understanding of the human mind (DV 6).[5]

Endnotes

1. The translation of *Dei Verbum* used in this book may be found by visiting the Vatican website www.vatican.va/archive/hist_councils/ii_vatican_council/ and clicking on the document name.

2. Inclusive language is used in this book with the exception of Bible quotations or church documents.

3. This excerpt from DV 5 contains note #4 as follows: 4. First Vatican Council, Dogmatic Constitution on the Catholic Faith, Chap. 3, "On Faith:" Denzinger 1789 (3008).

4. *Confessions of St. Augustine*, Book 8, trans. Rex Warner (New Jersey: Penguin Books, 1963), 181–83.

5. This excerpt from DV 6 contains note #5 as follows: 5. St. Jerome, Commentary on Isaiah, Prol.: PL 24,17. cf. Benedict XV, encyclical "Spiritus Paraclitus:" EB 475–480; Pius XII, encyclical "Divino Afflante Spiritu:" EB 544.

2

The Handing On of Divine Revelation

Often the Bible is thought of as one big book that has come down to us whole and entire, but it is not. What we have now is the end product of a long process that took shape by the contribution of many different individuals with distinctive experiences, influenced by what was happening in their world and time in history. Their stories were gradually written down, became books, and were eventually placed alongside other books. The result is a composite work such that the various parts do not always fit together perfectly—something like Grandma's crazy quilt. Sometimes there were two versions of the same speech or event. The final editors didn't discard one or the other but included both rather than lose any part of their sacred tradition.[1]

The complex process of writing the New Testament is examined in the Pontifical Biblical Commission's 1964 document, *Instruction on the Historical Truth of the Gospels*, which identifies three layers of tradition in the development of the Gospels:

1. **Jesus proclaims his message.** — The first layer is that of the historical Jesus, the words and deeds of a Palestinian Jew of the
   early first century. There is no evidence that Jesus ever wrote
   anything except his scribbling in the sand when asked to judge
   the woman accused of adultery (Jn 8:1–6). His teachings were
   given orally to the crowds who came to hear him preach and

heal. Jesus' proclamations attracted followers, but there were others who were opposed to him. Eventually he was arrested and condemned to death on a cross. When his disciples came to anoint his body they discovered an empty tomb.

2. **The disciples proclaim Jesus.** — The second layer consists of the oral preaching of the disciples. After Jesus rose from the dead, he commissioned his followers to communicate his good news (gospel) of salvation to all nations (Mt 28:19–20). In their preaching, by their example, and by their observances the disciples passed on what they received from Jesus, which they interpreted in light of his resurrection and its meaning for believers. The apostles and other disciples who carried the good news beyond Palestine to the cities of the gentile world had to adapt the message of Jesus to the customs, cultures, and languages of their audiences. Some stories and sayings of Jesus may have been written down and shared at this time.

3. **The evangelists record the message of Jesus.** — The final layer is the Gospels, which were written many years after the events they record and are the result of a long process of experience and reflection. The final texts show evidence that the evangelists (authors) used material that was already circulating in oral and written form. The church continues to transmit the full and living Gospel of Jesus, which is preserved by an "unending succession of preachers until the end of time" (DV 8). This process of handing on the living truth is called the "apostolic tradition."

What do Catholics mean by "Tradition"?

The dictionary defines "tradition" as the knowledge, doctrine, and practices transmitted from generation to generation. After Jesus' resurrection and ascension and the sending of the Holy Spirit at Pentecost, the disciples exercised the authority he gave them, faithfully handing on to their successors what had been taught. Paul writes in his letter to the church at Thessalonica, "So then, brothers and sisters, stand firm and hold fast to the traditions that you were taught by us, either by word of mouth or by our letter" (2 Thess 2:15).

When the apostles and the elders met in Jerusalem to judge whether or not Jewish laws were to be preserved in regard to the admission of gentiles into the church, the Old Testament did not give sufficient guidance in this matter.[2] Leaders of the community turned to the Holy Spirit, the living voice of Christ in the church, saying, "For it has seemed good to the Holy Spirit and to us to impose on you no further burden than these essentials" (Acts 15:28). The life of the church continues to be shaped by this oral tradition (Greek, *paradosis*, "handing on"), the living transmission of the sacred mystery of divine revelation.

Jews believe in a dual Torah—the written word in Scriptures and the oral word handed on and later preserved in the Mishnah and Talmud.[3] Rabbinic schools of the first century also developed what is called *midrashim*, books of commentary in which many perspectives of a text are recorded.[4] Similarly, Catholics do not base their faith on the Scriptures alone (*"sola scriptura"*) as some other Christians claim to do.[5] The church stresses that Scripture and tradition are interdependent: "Sacred tradition and Sacred Scripture form one sacred deposit of the Word of God, committed to the Church" (DV 2,10).

The word of God was transmitted to us both in an oral form (sacred tradition) and in a written form (sacred Scripture). The authentic, authoritative interpreter of this word of God is accomplished through the Holy Spirit in the church's teaching office, the Magisterium (the successor of St. Peter, the pope, and the bishops united to him). Through encyclicals, apostolic letters, exhortations, and other teachings, the church hands on to every generation all that she herself is and believes in her doctrine, life, and worship.

Tradition does not and cannot add anything to the words of Scripture, but tradition can and does reflect a deepening comprehension of the realities of which Scripture speaks. Tradition contains much that is not found explicitly in Scripture, such as theological teachings on the Trinity, the Eucharist, the papacy, the creed, doctrine, liturgical practices, and more. Jesus did not leave us an answer book for every possible situation the church might face in the future. What Jesus did leave the church was the guidance of the Holy Spirit. On the night before he died, Jesus told his followers:

I still have many things to say to you, but you cannot bear them now. When the Spirit of truth comes, he will guide you into all the truth; for he will not speak on his own, but will speak whatever he hears, and he will declare to you the things that are to come (Jn 16:12–13).

The Holy Spirit continually works in the church to adapt Christ's message to every age so that we have the assurance that what we are doing is essentially the same thing that every generation has done since Jesus. The word of God is not a museum piece; it is something alive. There is a growth in our understanding of what has been handed down to us. This happens through prayer and study, like Mary who "treasured all these words and pondered them in her heart" (Lk 2:19). *Dei Verbum* speaks of the continual unveiling of God's truth:

> For as the centuries succeed one another, the Church constantly moves forward toward the fullness of divine truth until the words of God reach their complete fulfillment in her (DV 8).

Endnotes

1. Compare the different versions of the creation story in the first two chapters of Genesis or Jesus' farewell address in chapters 14 and 16 of John's Gospel.
2. This gathering, often referred to as the "Jerusalem Council," was not a council in the modern sense of the word.
3. The Mishnah is the first part of the Talmud containing oral interpretations of scriptural ordinances compiled by the rabbis about 200 CE. The Talmud, which signifies both "learning" and "teaching," is a collection of writings completed between 400–600 CE. It contains two types of writing: *Halakhah* (Law) and *Haggadah* (story). The Talmud consists of two parts: the Mishnah (text) and the Gemara (commentary), but the term is sometimes restricted to the Gemara. Next to the Bible itself, the Talmud is the authoritative code for Jewish life.
4. An example of midrash is the story of Jonah as a commentary on what it means for Israel to be called a light to the nations. Midrash also fills in the missing pieces such as the infancy narratives in Matthew's and Luke's Gospels.
5. This maxim basically holds that the ultimate authority for Christians is the Bible alone and not the teaching church.

3

Sacred Scripture,
Its Inspiration
and Interpretation

What do Catholics mean by "divine inspiration"?

Dei Verbum has this to say about the inspiration of the Bible:

> For holy mother Church, relying on the belief of the Apostles (see John 20:31; 2 Tim. 3:16; 2 Peter 1:19–20, 3:15–16), holds that the books of both the Old and New Testaments in their entirety, with all their parts, are sacred and canonical because written under the inspiration of the Holy Spirit, they have God as their author and have been handed on as such to the Church herself (DV 11).[1]

The word "inspiration" means "God-breathed" or "divinely inspired" (Greek, *divinitus inspirata*). Paul writes to Timothy, a leader in the early church, "All scripture is inspired by God and is useful for teaching, for reproof, for correction, and for training in righteousness, so that everyone who belongs to God may be proficient, equipped for every good work" (2 Tim 3:16–17).

Until fairly recent times, inspiration was thought of as though the Holy Spirit dictated the biblical text word for word to the author. Human beings were just passive instruments of God with no creative powers of their own. During the last two centuries inspiration has been seen in a different light. We now understand that Paul did not take dictation from a divine voice as he wrote his letters. Inspired by the Spirit, he wrote in response to real situations that arose in the congregations that he visited and helped found. Eventually, the church came to realize that Paul's word to a particular community was also God's word to the whole church. *Dei Verbum* speaks of the human participation in writing Scripture:

> In composing the sacred books, God chose men and while employed by Him they made use of their powers and abilities, so that with Him acting in them and through them, they, as true authors, consigned to writing everything and only those things which He wanted (DV 11).[2]

If we ask who wrote the Bible, God or human beings, the answer is both. The Bible is the word of God expressed in the words of human beings. An analogy of this can be made to Jesus, the incarnate Word of God, who took on human flesh. So, too, the word of God in Scripture is "enfleshed" through human words. Divine inspiration occurred at every phase of the sacred Word, from the oral proclamation to the writing, collecting, and editing the text. God's word is a living word that continues to inspire the hearts of believers.

How do Catholics interpret sacred Scripture?

In the Acts of the Apostles, Philip overheard a man from Ethiopia reading a passage from the prophet Isaiah (53:7–8) and asked, "Do you understand what you are reading?" The man recognized his need for an interpreter and replied, "How can I, unless someone guides me?" (Acts 8:30–31). The process of interpretation continues today and asks questions from the contemporary world—philosophical, psychological, sociological, political, and so on. Of course, this makes the process more complex. At this point, the Ethiopian might have closed his book and given up!

As Catholics, we must faithfully seek a proper interpretation of Scripture in accordance with the teaching office of the church and with the aid of biblical scholars. This is not an easy task. One need only look at the history of Christianity to see the contradictory views held by the church fathers (the first interpreters of Scripture), the reformers, fundamentalists, and modern theologians. Consider the controversy that still persists about Jesus' words, "My flesh is true food and my blood is true drink" (Jn 6:55). Catholics believe that Jesus wasn't using symbolic or metaphorical language; he intended to say that his body and blood are real food and real drink. Jesus' followers also understood what he meant and some of them abandoned him because they could not accept what he said (6:59–66). Peter speaks about the necessity of competent assistance in the interpretation of Scripture:

> First of all you must understand this, that no prophecy of scripture is a matter of one's own interpretation, because no prophecy ever came by human will, but men and women moved by the Holy Spirit spoke from God (2 Pet 1:20–21).

In the past, Catholics were not always encouraged to read the Bible for fear of misinterpreting it. Following the Second Vatican Council, Catholics, eager to study the Bible, were sometimes drawn to radical liberalism that saw the Bible merely as a source of literary and historical knowledge to be studied as any other book. Others were attracted to the fundamentalist approach to Bible study that seems to supply easy answers to difficult questions. Fundamentalism is a movement that arose in 1895 by conservative Protestant scholars who believed in the literal meaning of Scripture and the Bible as the sole authority for the reader. A fundamentalist's method of reading the Bible without questioning and critical research is wrong. Fundamentalism refuses to admit that the word of God is expressed in human language by human authors who wrote in language and expressions that were conditioned by the culture and time in which they wrote. Fundamentalists insist that because the Bible is divinely inspired, it is inerrant, containing nothing that is factually untrue, and is absolutely free from error of any kind. For them, this applies not only to matters of faith but also to matters of history and science. *Dei Verbum* makes an important statement regarding the interpretation of Scripture:

> The books of Scripture must be acknowledged as teaching solidly, faithfully and without error that truth which God wanted put into sacred writings for the sake of salvation (DV 11).[3]

The emphasis must be placed on the words "for the sake of salvation." For Catholics, inerrancy of the Bible is relevant only insofar as it teaches us truth about God and God's plan for our lives. Biblical inerrancy does not pertain to those things that are not matters of salvation, such as history and science. Although the Bible contains some history and science, it is not to be read as a textbook. The authors of Scripture communicated truth through various styles, or literary forms, which cannot be understood by rational thought alone.

When reading the Bible it is important to ask critical questions. Was creation accomplished in seven days of twenty-four hours each? Or was the author trying to convey the power and ordered majesty of God's creation? Was the story of Noah and the Ark based on some event that really happened, or, more importantly, was the purpose to explain the ever-increasing wickedness of the human race? Did the author of Jonah intend us to believe that there was a fish large enough to swallow a human being? Or was the aim to show us how difficult it is to run away from God's call? Should we try to figure out which road the man took on the way to Jericho when he was accosted by robbers? Or was Jesus trying to teach us something about caring for others—even for those of different races or religious beliefs? Are the events described in the books of Daniel and Revelation intended to predict the future? Or do they convey messages of hope and faith in times of suffering and persecution? In reading the Bible we can't settle for simple answers to complex questions.

Someone once said, "All stories in the Bible are true, and some of them actually happened." Stories in the Bible are "true" even if they are not factual accounts of historical or scientific events. Poetry, allegory, proverbs, parables, songs, and stories convey deeper truths than the mere reciting of facts do. Biblical criticism takes into account the "literal" sense of Scripture while avoiding "literalism," a fundamentalist view of a text that has only one meaning as understood in English today.

What does "biblical criticism" mean?

The word "criticism" may sound negative. After all, who are we to criticize God's word? The term "criticism" as it applies to the study of Scripture does not mean faultfinding but rather detailed investigation and analysis. The contemporary method of biblical criticism is described by the Pontifical Biblical Commission's document *The Interpretation of the Bible in the Church* (1993). There are several methods that help us understand the complex process by which the sacred word came to us. While no single method adequately explains the richness of the biblical text, here are some we need to consider.

1. **The historical-critical** method is an indispensable approach that looks at the development behind the sacred text and the people to whom the biblical books were addressed in different places and in different times.

2. **Textual criticism** is the attempt to come as close to the original text as possible. We do not have the original text of any book of the Bible, and there are many differences in ancient biblical manuscripts, some due to copying errors, omissions, and insertions. By carefully comparing ancient manuscripts to each other, scholars try to establish the most correct wording.

3. **Literary criticism** is less concerned with the "who, what, why, when" questions of the historical-critical method. This approach asks, "What happens in the biblical narrative?" and "What do these events mean?"

4. **Liberation theology** considers the socio-economic, political circumstances of people. The Bible is read differently by minorities and poor and oppressed people in the Third World than it is by those living in well-to-do social classes of the First World. Feminist theology, a form of liberation theology, seeks to discover the status and equality of women that is often concealed in the writings of the Scriptures.

In addition to these methods, archaeological excavations and discoveries, such as the Dead Sea Scrolls, continue to shed light on the world in which the Bible was written.[4] In reading the Bible, it is important to pay attention to these perspectives, or "windows" into the biblical world.

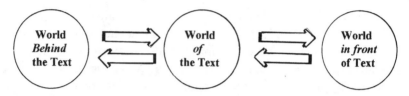

1. **The world** *behind* **the text:** What was it like "back then" and how do we know it?

2. **The world** *of* **the text:** What do the biblical authors think is important to emphasize?

3. **The world** *in front* **of the text:** What does the Bible mean to readers and hearers of the word today? How does it call us to conversion and transformation?

This may seem an impossible task, but we do something like this all the time. In reading a newspaper, we read the sports page differently than the way we read editorials, the comic strips, or the headlines. For example, what would future generations make of these captions from the sports page?

Cardinals Battle Devils

Sounds like the church leaders were doing their job!

St. Martha Beats St. Joseph

Pretty violent behavior for saints, don't you think? When we read these captions we automatically interpret them as the current sports jargon. We need to employ similar techniques when we read the Scriptures. Attention must be given to the language, idioms, and literary forms of biblical times that express truth in ways that are different than our own. *Dei Verbum* gives us some guidelines:

The interpreter of Sacred Scripture, in order to see clearly what God wanted to communicate to us, should carefully investigate what meaning the sacred writers really intended, and what God wanted to manifest by means of their words (DV 12).

Every time anyone reads the Bible, he or she automatically interprets it, reading through the "lens," the particular beliefs and values, of his or her own place and time. Even those who claim to take the Bible literally are interpreting what they read. If a person believes that every word in the Bible is literally true, he or she will read the Bible one way. And if a person believes that the Bible is truthful without having to be an historical document, he or she will read it another way.

While the Pontifical Biblical Commission affirms the importance of the historical-critical method as useful and necessary, Catholic scholars must never forget that what they are interpreting is the word of God. Their task is not finished when they determine what the words of Scripture meant *then*. They must also ask what the text means *now*.[5] They arrive at their true goal only when they explain the meaning of the biblical text in a way that provides spiritual nourishment for everyone who reads it.

Endnotes

1. This excerpt from DV 11 contains note #1 as follows: cf. First Vatican Council, Dogmatic Constitution on the Catholic Faith, Chap. 2 "On Revelation:" Denzinger 1787 (3006); Biblical Commission, Decree of June 18, 1915: Denzinger 2180 (3629): EB 420; Holy Office, Epistle of Dec. 22, 1923: EB 499.

2. This excerpt from DV 11 contains notes #2, #3, and #4 as follows: 2. cf. Pius XII, encyclical "Divino Afflante Spiritu," Sept. 30, 1943: A.A.S. 35 (1943) p. 314; Enchiridion Bible. (EB) 556. 3. "In" and "for" man: cf. Heb. 1, and 4, 7; ("in"): 2 Sm. 23,2; Matt. 1:22 and various places; ("for"): First Vatican Council, Schema on Catholic Doctrine, note 9: Coll. Lac. VII, 522. 4. Leo XIII, encyclical "Providentissimus Deus," Nov. 18, 1893: Denzinger 1952 (3293); EB 125.

3. This excerpt from DV 11 contains note #5 as follows: 5. cf. St. Augustine, "Gen. ad Litt." 2, 9, 20: PL 34, 270–271; Epistle 82, 3: PL 33, 277: CSEL 34, 2, p. 354. St. Thomas, "On Truth," Q. 12, A. 2, C. Council of Trent, session IV, Scriptural Canons: Denzinger 783 (1501). Leo XIII, encyclical "Providentissimus Deus:" EB 121, 124, 126–127. Pius XII, encyclical "Divino Afflante Spiritu:" EB 539.

4. The Dead Sea Scrolls are a library of manuscripts found in 1947 in the monastery at Qumran, Israel. They contain manuscripts from the surrounding community (perhaps the Essenes) and Hebrew and Greek texts of most of the Bible including the apocrypha.

5. Biblical hermeneutics is a method of interpretation that strives to understand the text in contemporary terms. The term "hermeneutics" comes from Hermes, the Greek messenger god, and means "interpretation." An example of this analysis is the line from John 18:38, when Pilate asks, "What is truth?" Were these words spoken cynically, contemptuously, longingly? How would people understand Pilate's question today?

Understanding the Old Testament

T he Old Testament presents a history of the Hebrew people from their earliest stages to their formation into a community of faith and their downfall in exile in Babylon. But the Old Testament is much more than history. In it one can learn about God's plan for all of humankind, especially the chosen people, the Jews. The Old Testament is primarily a faith record of a people whose triumphs and defeats were interpreted as God's action on their behalf. These stories were told and retold by word of mouth from one generation to the next and reinterpreted in light of ever-changing circumstances. Eventually, these stories were written down.

The first five books of the Bible—Genesis, Exodus, Leviticus, Numbers, and Deuteronomy—form a distinct group known as the *Torah*, the "Law" or "instruction." The Torah is the founding charter of the nation of Israel. Parts of these books of Scripture were probably first compiled around 1000 BCE, during the time of the monarchy, but they deal with events that took place many hundreds of years before that time. *Dei Verbum* has this to say of the Hebrew Bible:

> These same books, then, give expression to a lively sense of God, contain a store of sublime teachings about God, sound wisdom about human life, and a wonderful treasury of prayers, and in them the mystery of our salvation is present in a hidden way. Christians should receive them with reverence (DV 15).

The Old Testament can and should be read in its own right, yet
Christians tend to read the biblical text with "Christological" eyes to
discover the person of Jesus and the events concerning him. At the
same time, there is another layer of meaning, a "fuller sense" (Latin,
sensus plenior) of the text that was intended by God but not clearly
expressed by the human author. When Hosea wrote, "Out of Egypt I
called my son" (Hos 11:1b), he probably was thinking of the
deliverance of God's people at the time of the Exodus. Matthew
quoted this verse concerning Jesus, who returned from Egypt as a
child after the death of Herod (Mt 2:15). For Christians, the books of
the Old Testament prepare us for the coming of Jesus Christ and the
kingdom of God that he proclaimed. St. Augustine saw an intimate
relationship between the two testaments:

> There is nothing in the New Testament that is not foreshadowed in the
> Old Testament, and there is nothing in the Old Testament that is not
> revealed in the New Testament.

The whole Bible, both the Old and New Testaments, can be read
as the development of a set of themes that recur again and again
throughout the entire Bible.

Creation

God the creator called all things into being by the all-powerful
word: "Then God said, 'Let there be light'; and there was light"
(Gen 1:3). The seventh day of creation was the day of God's rest, the
Sabbath (Hebrew, shabbat, "to cease"), a reminder for all humankind
to stop their labors and rest with the Lord. It was not simply for their
own mental and physical health that the people refrained from work.
The Sabbath was a day when they remembered the mighty things God
had done on their behalf, but it also was a charge to keep that day
holy.

The creation story establishes a world of relationships, human
partnership with God, with one another, and with all created beings
(see Ps 104). Men and women are created in God's image (Latin,
Imago Dei). They are given "dominion" (Gen 1:26), not
"domination," to care for one another and all creation. The stories of

creation are not intended to be scientific or historical descriptions of the origins of things but theological interpretations that reveal the deepest truth. They are the kind of stories that all peoples tell, such as the great epic poem *Enuma Elish* written by the Babylonians. It tells how their chief god Marduk created the world in a bloody battle, and how Ea, the god of water, saved humanity from the flood. In the *Gilgamesh* epic, the hero of the story journeyed to the bottom of the sea to obtain a tree that would guarantee eternal life. On his way home, a hungry snake snatched the plant from him. It was a sign to Gilgamesh that old age and death was the fate of human beings, so he gave up and went home.

The biblical authors reworked these ancient stories to understand the problem of good and evil in the world. For the author of Genesis, the one true God created heaven and earth, not by some cosmic battle but by a powerful word. There was a tree of life, not at the bottom of the sea but in the center of a garden and available to all.

Sin

The word most frequently used in the Bible to signify failure or fault is the Greek word *hamartia* (Hebrew, *chata'*), which means "to miss the mark." Adam and Eve personified the human race in their willful disobedience that we name "original sin," the individual and corporate condition of sin that prevents human beings from enjoying a right relationship with God. The story of Cain killing his brother Abel was a prototype for the spiraling of violence between families, tribes, and nations found throughout the Bible. There was no remedy for sin except for God's mercy and forgiveness.

In the New Testament, Jesus is the "new Adam" whose obedience to God's will in the garden of Gethsemane is the counterpart of Adam's willful disobedience. At the end of the Bible, in the Book of Revelation, we return to the garden, the "new Eden," where the tree no longer brings the curse of death for sin (Rev 22:2). For Catholics, the sacrament of penance, or confession, is a means of God's grace that gives us strength to overcome sin in our lives:

If we confess our sins, he who is faithful and just will forgive us our sins and cleanse us from all unrighteousness (1 Jn 1:9).

God's Call

Regardless of their failure to obey God's will, the people of Israel were conscious of being God's chosen people: "For you are a people holy to the LORD your God; the LORD your God has chosen you out of all the peoples on earth to be his people, his treasured possession" (Deut 7:6).

Being chosen, or elected, by God did not mean that they were the smartest, bravest, or most faithful people God could find. Nor did being chosen mean the exclusion of other nations and peoples. God told the prophet Isaiah, "I will give you as a light to the nations, that my salvation may reach to the end of the earth" (Isa 49:6b).

Throughout the Bible, God called individuals irrespective of their abilities or personal worthiness. God called Abraham (the first patriarch in the Bible, followed by his son Isaac and grandson Jacob) and asked him to give up everything—land and family—in order to follow God's call and to move to an unfamiliar land and unknown future. Despite the sad fact was that Abraham's wife, Sarah, was unable to bear children, God promised him descendants as numerous as the sand on the shore or the stars in the sky.[1]

Abraham's destination was a land called Canaan, later known as Israel. This narrow strip of land within the Fertile Crescent, not more than 120 miles long by 40 miles wide, was the Promised Land, described as a "land flowing with milk and honey" (Ex 3:8). What made Canaan important was its location between Mesopotamia to the north and Egypt to the south, flanked by the Mediterranean Sea on the west and a vast expanse of desert to the east. Canaan was a natural bridge over which traders and superpowers paraded. Abraham's response to God's call was one of trust and obedience, what the Bible calls "faith," a quality admired by believers throughout the ages. It is by faith that all who believe in Christ are called and find salvation in baptism.

Salvation

Salvation is one of the over-arching themes in both testaments. The Hebrew word for "salvation" is yasha, literally, "to open wide." God opened a way through the sea and a way through the desert as

God's people traveled to the Promised Land. The liberation of the Hebrew people from slavery in Egypt was the key to understanding salvation. When people wanted to understand other saving events, they turned to the Exodus.

Moses is the central figure in the Book of Exodus. From the moment he was born, his life was a journey of peril. Moses' mother defied Pharaoh's command to slay all Hebrew infants, and in desperation she set her child adrift on the sea. He was drawn from the waters by Pharaoh's own daughter—foreshadowing Israel's deliverance through the Red Sea. Although raised in the luxury of the Egyptian court, Moses encountered God in an ordinary bush aflame with the divine presence. He was chosen by God to go to Pharaoh and demand that the slaves be set free. To overcome Moses' objections that he was unworthy of the task, God told him, "I will be with you" (Ex 3:12). In saying this, God's mysterious name was revealed: "I AM WHO I AM" (3:14, in Hebrew, *Yahweh*), which can mean: "I AM the one who called into existence," the One who cannot be named or defined.

For Christians, salvation is not just an event but a person whose name is Jesus, *Yeshua*, a form of "Joshua," which means "God is salvation" (see Mt 1:21). Christians interpret the life of Christ and all of the Christian life as an exodus. Jesus is our new Moses, our liberator, savior, and mediator of the covenant with God.

Covenant

God's covenant is a major theme found throughout the Old and New Testaments. In ancient times there were pacts or agreements made between individuals, clans, tribes, cities, and nations, which were binding to both parties. These covenants were not always written documents; solemn words or rituals often ratified them. The terms and obligations of the covenant were similar to other ancient Near East treaties and contracts. God promised to protect Israel from harm and bring about their deliverance. Israel in turn promised to obey God's words in worship and conduct.

The first covenant in the Bible was made with Noah (Gen 9:1–17), and the sign of fulfillment was a rainbow, which was a sign of peace and not an instrument of war. The covenant made with Noah was intended for all humankind—*Berît Olam*, an "everlasting covenant" for all generations.

The Hebrew word for covenant is *berît*, "to cut," an expression still used in business transactions—"to cut a deal." This idea is seen in the ratification of the covenant with Abraham based on an ancient ceremonial rite (15:1–21). When two parties entered a covenant, they would walk between the slain carcasses of birds and animals, saying in effect, "May this be done to you and me if the covenant is broken."

The sign of the covenant was circumcision (Hebrew, *brit-milah*, 17:10–14), which was mandatory for every Hebrew male. This sign in the flesh represented the hope of the Hebrew people that they and their descendants would possess the land according to the promise that God made to Abraham. God was not interested in only an outward ritual but in inward transformation, a circumcision of the heart (Deut 30:6).

The word that best expresses God's covenant-love with Israel is *hesed*, God's mercy and forgiveness despite human infidelity. When Israel broke the covenant, God made provisions for its renewal sealed in the sacrificial blood splashed on the altar and on the people by Moses. This cultic ritual symbolically stated that both God and the people pledged themselves to the endurance of the covenant. In the New Testament, Jesus sealed the covenant in his blood sacrifice on the cross. Jesus' dying and rising accomplished what the Law could not do.

Law

Of several law codes surviving from the ancient Middle East, the most famous is the Code of Hammurabi, king of Babylon in 2500 BCE. It was carved on a stone stele (an engraved pillar) to publicly proclaim his laws so that his people might know what was required of them. Immoral acts such as murder, adultery, and false charges were severely denounced. This code has many parallels to the biblical Torah. In its grim penalties we can see where the Hebrews learned the law of retaliation (lex talionis), which prescribed proportional punishment. The Code of Hammurabi stated that if a man destroyed the eye of another man, they could destroy his eye. If a man broke another man's bone, they could break his bone. The Law given on

Sinai declared in the case of serious injury, "then you shall give life for life, eye for eye, tooth for tooth, hand for hand, foot for foot, burn for burn, wound for wound, stripe for stripe" (Ex 21:23–25). The existence of this code and others like it demonstrates that Israel shared with her neighbors an ideal of justice that would be administered by a righteous ruler.

In the Book of Exodus God's people were bound together in a mutual contract, or covenant, on Mount Sinai. The Ten Commandments (Ex 20:1–17; Deut 5:6–21) are a summary of divine and human wisdom, reasonable rules to guide human conduct, and the basis of a free and just society. The first three laws were directed to the people's relationship with God, and the next seven referred to their relationship with their brothers and sisters. These laws were founded on love, not only prohibitions.

When Moses brought God's Law before the people, they answered as one: "Everything that the LORD has spoken we will do" (Ex 19:8). In reality they could not obey even the first command as proved by their worship of the "golden calf" (32:1–4).

In Jesus' Sermon on the Mount (Mt 5—7), he is portrayed as a new Moses who did not come to do away with the Law but to fulfill it. For Jews and Christians, the law is not oppressive if responded to with love and fidelity:

> I do not turn away from your ordinances, for you have taught me. How sweet are your words to my taste, sweeter than honey to my mouth! (Ps 119:102–103).

Banquet

The Bible sets before us a banquet of divine wisdom that satisfies our deepest human hungers. The psalmist writes:

> You prepare a table before me in the presence of my enemies; you anoint my head with oil; my cup overflows. Surely goodness and mercy shall follow me all the days of my life, and I shall dwell in the house of the LORD my whole life long (23:5–6).

The Passover meal is the celebration of Israel's liberation from slavery in Egypt. In their struggle for independence in the Exodus, the people sought a life of human dignity and personal freedom whereby they could worship the one true God. The word "Passover" is taken from God's instructions to the Hebrew slaves, who were to sprinkle the blood of a lamb on the doorposts of their homes:

> The blood shall be a sign for you on the houses where you live: when I see the blood, I will pass over you, and no plague shall destroy you when I strike the land of Egypt (Ex 12:13).

Today, our Jewish brothers and sisters repeat the Exodus story to their children within the context of the Passover Seder meal. In their annual retelling of this story of affliction and deliverance, the Jews not only tell a story from the past, it becomes part of their present lives. The people must remember (Hebrew, *zakar*) what God had done for them in the past. At the same time, the Passover expresses hope in a future when all people will live in freedom from hunger and thirst: "On this mountain the LORD of hosts will make for all peoples a feast of rich food, a feast of well-aged wines" (Isa 25:6).

This messianic banquet is anticipated in Jesus' multiplication of the loaves and fish in the wilderness. The long-awaited Messiah was expected to be a prophet like Moses who fed the people in the desert with miraculous "manna" from heaven. Jesus said to those who followed him:

> I am the bread of life. Whoever comes to me will never be hungry, and whoever believes in me will never be thirsty (Jn 6:35).

At Passover, Jesus shared his last supper with his disciples before his passion and death, and said:

> "Take, eat; this is my body." Then he took a cup, and after giving thanks he gave it to them, saying, "Drink from it, all of you; for this is my blood of the covenant, which is poured out for many for the forgiveness of sins" (Mt 26:26–28).

After Christ's death and resurrection, Christians gathered to share his body and blood in the eucharistic banquet, as they continue to do today in expectation of the eternal celebration in heaven.

The Promised Land

After the Exodus, Moses' successor Joshua told the people that if they were to possess the land, they must commit themselves unreservedly to the covenant of the one true God, saying, "As for me and my household, we will serve the LORD (Josh 24:15b). Acceptance of the covenant changed the people from separate wandering tribes to a community bound to one another with God as their leader. When Joshua and the people crossed the river Jordan, it stopped flowing. Then the priests carried the Ark of the Covenant into the Promised Land. This was the portable shrine containing the tablets of the Ten Commandments that traveled with Moses and the people throughout their desert wanderings. Israel would dwell in security in the land if they were faithful to God and the covenant; if they were unfaithful the land would be lost.

After the Hebrew people entered the Promised Land, God raised up tribal heroes called "judges" (spiritual military leaders) to lead the people. Whenever the people lapsed into sin, their enemies punished them. When they cried out in repentance, God sent a judge such as Deborah, Gideon, or Samson to save them. Throughout the Book of Judges the cycle of sin-punishment-repentance-salvation occurs again and again. God's mercy is unlimited when people truly repent (Hebrew, *teshuvah*, Greek, *metanoia*, to "turn back"). But the Book of Judges ends with a dire statement of unrepentance: "In those days there was no king in Israel; all the people did what was right in their own eyes" (Judg 21:25).

Kingdom

After the period of the judges, the leader of the nation was Samuel, who was not only a judge but also a prophet and priest. There was a growing feeling that Israel should have a king who would weld the nation into a unified whole and command an army that could protect them, especially from the warring, sea-faring Philistines. Samuel objected to the people's demand for a king. Israel was not like other nations; Israel already had a ruler, who was the Lord. Although he pointed out that a king would make heavy demands on the people, they insisted. Their punishment? They got a king!

Samuel anointed Saul as king, and at first God's favor was with Saul as he led the nation to victory. However, Saul disobeyed God's command and fell into disfavor. The king of Israel was not above the law, but was bound by the covenant as any other Israelite. Samuel declared that God would designate a new king, a man after God's "own heart" (1 Sam 13:14).

God's favor rested on David, who was anointed king by Samuel. Under David and his son Solomon, Israel reached its zenith as a political power. The nation was united, secure, well defended and was even able to expand. About the year 1000 BCE, David captured the city of Jerusalem and made it his capital, the "City of David." Then David brought the Ark of the Covenant to Jerusalem, and the city became the religious center of Israel as well. When David decided to build a permanent dwelling place for God, he was surprised to hear that God had other plans. It was God who would build a house for David and his heirs unconditionally and forever (2 Sam 7:16). Christians see this promise fulfilled in the eternal kingship of Jesus Christ.

Division

During the peaceful, prosperous time of David and Solomon, the people reflected on their stories and traditions and began to write their sacred history. The First Book of Kings describes Solomon's role in building the magnificent Temple in Jerusalem and his legendary wisdom. Yet Solomon made some unwise decisions. He established social classes of the rich and poor. His intermarriage with foreign wives introduced pagan worship right in the Temple courts. Solomon's weaknesses and excesses eventually led to the nation's downfall.

After Solomon's death in 922 BCE, the nation fell apart. The northern tribes of Israel formed an independent kingdom to rival the southern kingdom of Judah. The united kingdom lasted less than one hundred years. The downward spiraling of sin told in the stories in

Genesis is repeated in the dark story of the kings of Israel and their unfaithfulness to the Law of Moses. With the exception of kings Hezekiah and Josiah, they ignored the covenant, and the Canaanite religion, especially worship of the god Baal, became widely practiced among the people.

It was a prophet, not a king, who emerged as a major personality during this time. Elijah's whole prophetic career was spent in opposition to the idolatry and corruption of the northern kingdom of Israel. On Mount Carmel, Elijah had a contest with the prophets of Baal and he defeated them (1 Kings 17—18). The vengeful queen Jezebel forced Elijah to flee for his life, and he hid in terror in a cave on Mount Horeb (also known as Sinai). There God appeared to the prophet, not in a great wind, earthquake, or fire as in God's appearance to Moses but in the "sound of sheer silence" (19:12). God asked, "What are you doing here, Elijah?" (19:13). One cannot prophesy in a mountain cave, and before he was mysteriously taken up to heaven, Elijah passed his prophet's mantel on to Elisha. To this day, orthodox Jews expect the return of Elijah at Passover.

During this period the prophet Amos condemned Israel's social injustice and religious complacency: "Let justice roll down like waters, and righteousness like an ever-flowing stream" (5:24). Hosea foretold political disaster if they refused to return to the Lord (11:1–5). The prophet Micah chastised the rich exploiters of the poor, giving them a one-line summary of God's requirements: "He has told you, O mortal, what is good; and what does the LORD require of you but to do justice, and to love kindness, and to walk humbly with your God" (6:8).

During the reign of Josiah (640–609 BCE), a copy of the book of the Law (probably Deuteronomy) was found in the Temple while it was being repaired. When the book was read to the king, Josiah rent his garments and had the book read out loud to all the people gathered in the Temple, reminding them of the covenant: "Hear, O Israel: The LORD is our God, the LORD alone. You shall love the LORD your God with all your heart, and with all your soul, and with all your might" (Deut 6:4–5).

This prayer, called the *Shema* (a command meaning "hear"), is the basic principle of the whole Mosaic Law and remains so today. The Lord alone is deserving of undivided devotion. Sadly Josiah's reign ended in tragedy when he was killed on the plains of Megiddo in a battle between the king of Egypt and the king of Assyria. Although there were brief periods of independence, the tiny country of Israel became subject to one empire after another. "**E**at **A**t **B**en's, **P**alestine's **G**reatest **R**estaurant" is a simple way to memorize these nations: Egypt, Assyria, Babylon, Persia, Greece, and Rome.

Assyrian Invasion

Assyria originated in what is now northern Iraq near the Tigris River, and it grew to be one of the major empires in the ancient Near East. When the northern kingdom of Israel joined revolts against Assyria, they paid the price by being invaded. In 721 BCE the capital city Samaria fell and many of its citizens were deported. Known as the "ten lost tribes of Israel," they were eventually absorbed by various nations. In addition, a large number of captured people from other lands were brought to Israel, and there was some intermarriage resulting in a mixed population called the "Samaritans."

The prophet Isaiah implored Judah to have confidence that God would act to save them from their enemies and restore peace to the land: "They shall beat their swords into plowshares, and their spears into pruning hooks; nation shall not lift up sword against nation, neither shall they learn war any more (Isa 2:4b). Despite the prophet's urging, the kingdom of Judah feared the Assyrians more than they trusted God. Yet in time, the Assyrian Empire grew weaker and finally collapsed. In 612 BCE the Assyrian capital of Nineveh fell.

Babylonian Exile

The kingdom of Judah survived, but in 587 BCE it too was invaded, this time by the Babylonians under King Nebuchadnezzar. Solomon's Temple was destroyed and the king and leading citizens were taken into exile. Zedekiah, the last king of Judah, watched as his sons were killed. Then he was blinded and taken in chains to Babylon. The psalmist laments, "How could we sing the LORD's song in a foreign land?" (Ps 137:4).

The disaster posed a real problem for the faith of Israel. To all appearances, God had broken the covenant or else was not able to keep it. God promised a land, and the people were in exile. God promised that David's line would last forever, and the king was deported. Was Marduk, the god of Babylon, more powerful than Yahweh, the God of Israel? In the darkest of times, the prophets became the spiritual leaders and critical conscience of Israel. The prophets reminded the people of their past unfaithfulness to God's covenant but also of God's fidelity in the future.

With the Temple destroyed and the ancient sacrificial worship taken from them, the synagogue became the heart of each Jewish community, the gathering place for prayer and the study of Scripture. The pilgrimage feasts, once celebrated in Jerusalem, were now observed in the home. A scribal class emerged whose task was to interpret the sacred Scripture. Israel's history, traditions, and laws were collected and codified. The Torah—the Law, the Prophets, and the Writings—became the center of Israel's life as a people.

During this period, the wise men of Israel, called "sages," reflected on the human condition. The mystery of pain and evil is seen in the Book of Job and Israel's grief and confession of guilt is emphasized in the Book of Lamentations. The Exile was understood not as the Lord's rejection but as punishment for sin. Despite their affliction, Israel hoped in God's forgiveness and restoration.

Persian Rule

In 539 BCE, Cyrus the Great, king of Persia, conquered the Babylonian Empire and established the largest empire the world had yet known. Isaiah regarded Cyrus as a "messiah" because he liberated the exiles in Babylon, the only time in Scripture that a foreigner is called God's "anointed" (Isa 45:1). In 538 Cyrus exhorted the exiles to return to their ancestral land to rebuild their Temple. The Hebrew canon of Scriptures ends with the edict of Cyrus:

> Thus says King Cyrus of Persia: "The LORD, the God of heaven, has given me all the kingdoms of the earth, and he has charged me to build him a house at Jerusalem, which is in Judah. Whoever is among you of all his people, may the LORD his God be with him! Let him go up" (2 Chr 36:23).

When the exiles returned home, they were under the rule of the Persian Empire. Two important figures emerged in this period: Ezra, a priest, and Nehemiah, a Persian court official. Each helped to maintain Jewish identity during the difficult struggle of restoration. Under their leadership the Temple was rebuilt in 515 BCE. Ezra reminded the people that their first loyalty was to the covenant of God, not the nation, and their chief goal was to keep the Law of Moses. Ezra's dedication to the Law earned him the title "father of Judaism." Ever after, Judaism would be centered on the Law and the Jews would be called "the people of the book."

Greek and Roman Rule

For two centuries, the Persian Empire ruled Israel. By 400 BCE Persia's power began to weaken while the strength of Greece grew. The Persian Empire came to an end with the conquests of Alexander the Great (336–323). Alexander not only wanted political control of these vast territories, he also wanted to unite the empire with Greek culture, known as Hellenism or "Greek-ism," principally expressed in its language, literature, philosophy, and art. A new era had begun, which meant drastic changes for people in all parts of the world, including the people of Israel.

After Alexander's death, his kingdom was divided between the Seleucid dynasty in Syria and the Ptolemaic dynasty in Egypt. At first the Jews were left to govern their own internal affairs. This policy changed radically under Antiochus Epiphanes IV, king of Syria (165–161 BCE), who attempted to force the Jews to abandon the customs of their ancestors and the laws of God. Antiochus's greatest crime was the desecration of the Temple when he decreed that a statue of Zeus be worshiped in the sanctuary and unclean animals be sacrificed on the altar of burnt offering.

This abomination, told in the Book of Daniel (11:31), triggered the bloody Maccabean[2] revolt. In 164 BCE, after three years of struggle against incredible odds, the Jews succeeded in throwing off the yoke of foreign rule. For the first time since the divided kingdom some 500 years earlier, the Jews tasted military success and religious freedom. The Temple was cleansed and the Jews gathered in joy to celebrate its rededication. The lamps of dedication miraculously burned for eight days, even though the Maccabees had enough oil to last only one day. Jews today commemorate this event with the lighting of the menorah, the eight-branched candlestick, on Hanukkah ("dedication," 2 Macc 10:5—8), also called the Feast of Lights.

For a brief period of time, the Jews gained independence under the Hasmonean Dynasty (descendants of Simon Maccabeus), but this freedom did not last. The Hasmoneans soon became as corrupt as their oppressors. When the Romans were asked to settle a dispute in 63 BCE, the Roman general Pompey came to Jerusalem and put an end to their independence. Once again, the Jews served a foreign master, this time the mighty republic of Rome. In 69 BCE, Vespasian, who was later crowned emperor, was dispatched to Palestine to crush a full-scale Jewish revolt (66–70 CE). Titus, his son and successor, ended the revolt by destroying the city and the Temple in 70 CE.

Again the people wondered if God had cast them off. Perhaps they recalled the words of the prophet Micah during the Babylonian Exile. He gave hope to the people by announcing a future ruler who would come from David's birthplace in Bethlehem to rule in Israel and restore the covenant (Mic 5:1–5). How? The answer did not lie in the vision of the prophet. It awaited the coming of a savior, the anointed Son of God.

Endnotes

1. Abraham was originally called "Abram." His name change to Abraham expanded the meaning from "exalted father" to ab-hamon goyim, "father of a host of nations," the spiritual ancestor of Jews, Christians, and Muslims.

2. Judas, surnamed Maccabeus (Greek, "hammer"), was the third son of Mattathias and the leader of the Jewish resistance against Antiochus Epiphanes. The name Maccabees was applied to all the sons and to the Maccabean revolt they led. Emerging in Jewish thought, and of importance to Christians, is the idea of praying for the dead (2 Macc 12:44), and the resurrection to new life (7:9), which is brought out in the second Book of Maccabees.

5

Understanding the
New Testament

In contrast to the long period of composition of the Old
Testament, the books of the New Testament were composed in a
relatively shorter time (circa 50–110 CE). The New Testament,
like its predecessor the Old Testament, was not formed in a vacuum.
It evolved out of the shared experience of a body of believers who were
already proclaiming the gospel before any written document appeared.
It was the church that decided which of the many writings circulating
in the first century were clearly canonical or "sacred Scripture."

The first writings of the New Testament were not the Gospels but
the epistles. The earliest document we have is Paul's letter to the
Thessalonians, composed around 49–50 CE.[1] Paul, a strictly observant
Jew and a Roman citizen, was intent on keeping the Law of Moses
until he met the risen Christ as he set out to persecute Christians (Acts
9:1–5).[2] When Christ appeared to him and asked, "Why do you
persecute me?" (9:4), Paul came to understand the church as the
"Body of Christ" (1 Cor 12:27). By persecuting the church, Paul was
persecuting Christ. Paul stressed the equality of all those who were
baptized in Christ:

> As many of you as were baptized into Christ have clothed yourselves
> with Christ. There is no longer Jew or Greek, there is no longer slave or
> free, there is no longer male and female; for all of you are one in Christ
> Jesus (Gal 3:27–28).

After Paul's transformation "in Christ," he was sent to preach the good news to the gentiles (non-Jews), to "bring salvation to the ends of the earth" (Acts 13:47b). At a later date, between 70 and 110, the Gospels were composed from the many traditions that had circulated orally or in written form from the time of Jesus.

What is a Gospel?

The word "gospel" is derived from the Anglo-Saxon word *God-Spiel*, meaning "good tidings" (Greek, *euangélion*, "to announce good news"). The word "gospel" did not originally designate a book but a proclamation of a significant event such as a victory or a king's ascent to the throne. The prophet Isaiah gave the word its religious meaning when he announced the "good news" of Israel's deliverance from exile: "How beautiful upon the mountains are the feet of the messenger who announces peace, who brings good news, who announces salvation, who says to Zion, 'Your God reigns'" (Isa 52:7).

In the New Testament the word "gospel," or "good news," has a specifically Christian meaning, as seen in Mark's opening verse of his Gospel: "The beginning of the good news [gospel] of Jesus Christ, the Son of God" (Mk 1:1). In a synagogue in Nazareth, Jesus announced the good news that God's reign of healing, love, and mercy was fulfilled in him:

> The Spirit of the Lord is upon me, because he has anointed me to bring good news to the poor. He has sent me to proclaim release to the captives and recovery of sight to the blind, to let the oppressed go free, to proclaim the year of the Lord's favor (Lk 4:18–19).

The Gospels are the heart and center of the Christian Bible, a faith record and an invitation to meet the Lord. Like Judaism, Christianity did not come into being in response to a book. The first Christians responded to the manifestation of God's words and works in the person of Jesus Christ. As the Christian communities grew and matured they were less interested in the historical Jesus than they were in the Christ of faith.

Jesus of History

To understand the historical Jesus, we need to look at the human person of Jesus. It is important to remember that Jesus lived in a very different culture than our own and, in his human nature, was very much a person of his own historical time. If we wish to understand him and his message, we must become familiar with the world in which he lived. According to the Scriptures he was born in Bethlehem, but people knew him as "Jesus of Nazareth," the town in Galilee where he grew up. His name in English, Jesus (Greek, *Iesous*), was derived from the Hebrew *Yeshua*, meaning "Yahweh saves." Jesus spoke Aramaic, a Semitic language widely spoken from the time of the Exile. He also read and spoke Hebrew, the sacred language of the Scriptures and the synagogue, and perhaps some Greek. To facilitate understanding of the liturgical texts written in Hebrew, there was the Targum, an Aramaic paraphrase of the Bible. For Jesus and his contemporaries the Bible was not considered the "Old Testament"; it was simply the "Scriptures," the Law and the Prophets (Mt 5:17; Lk 24:27) and the Holy Writings.

As a Jew of the Semitic race, Jesus probably had black hair, dark eyes, and olive-colored skin. Although we are interested in what Jesus looked like, the biblical authors were more interested in what Jesus *did*. As an infant Jesus was circumcised and presented to God in the Temple of Jerusalem, rebuilt by Herod the Great (37 BCE–4 CE). When he was twelve years old, the age of responsibility, he was counted among the ten males (*minyan*) in his community necessary for public prayer in the synagogue. When Jesus went to Jerusalem with his parents to celebrate the Passover, he lingered behind in the Temple, "sitting among the teachers, listening to them and asking them questions" (Lk 2:46b). Like any other child, Jesus did not fully understand who he was. As he grew "in wisdom and in years" (2:52), he had a growing consciousness that he was God's Son.

As an adult, Jesus was a male celibate who practiced the trade of a carpenter (Greek, *tekton*, "craftsman") at Nazareth, where he lived. As a Jew, Jesus observed all the religious feasts, practices, and institutions of Judaism. Three times a year he went to Jerusalem to observe the Jewish high feasts (Ex 34:23; Deut 16:16). These "pilgrimage feasts" are:

1. **Passover** (Hebrew, *Pesach*, also "Feast of Unleavened Bread") takes its name from the meal shared at the time of the Exodus, when the angel of death "passed over" the Hebrew slaves whose houses were marked with the blood of the paschal lamb.

2. **Pentecost** (Hebrew, *Shevuot*, also "Feast of Weeks") takes its name from the fact that it was celebrated on the fiftieth day (Greek, *pentekoste*) after Passover. It was a time of prayer in thanksgiving for a good harvest and later became the annual memorial of the covenant given on Sinai.

3. **Tabernacles** (Hebrew, *Sukkot*, also "Feast of Booths") takes its name from the huts in which people camped during the harvest and those built in Jerusalem throughout the seven days of the feast. The booths also reminded the Jews of the tents the Hebrew people erected during their wandering in the desert after the Exodus.

Judaism in the time of Jesus did not constitute a uniform religion. There were a number of religious movements and parties within Judaism:

1. **The Pharisees** (meaning the "separated ones") were laymen who were staunch upholders of both the Mosaic Law and the oral tradition, including 613 rules and regulations, each relating to one basic detail of the Law. The Pharisees alone of all the religious parties survived the destruction of Jerusalem in 70 CE. They are the forerunners of Rabbinical Judaism.

2. **The Sadducees** were mostly priests and aristocrats, supporters of the established order and collaborators with the Romans. Unlike the Pharisees, the written Law alone was normative for the Sadducees. They did not await the coming of the Messiah, and they rejected belief in angels and the resurrection of the dead.

3. **The Scribes** were the official interpreters of the Scriptures and its oral traditions, applying the Law to daily life. In the New Testament they are also called "lawyers" who aligned themselves with the Pharisees.

4. **The Essenes** (from the Hebrew *hasin*, the "pious ones") considered themselves a remnant of true Judaism. Hostile to the Tem-

ple priesthood, the Essenes withdrew from society to live in a monastic community at Qumran near the Dead Sea. They lived an ascetic lifestyle and awaited the coming of the "teacher of righteousness" who would restore true worship.

5. **The Zealots** were not a religious sect but militant nationalists. Their fanatical terrorist acts in 66 CE provoked Roman repression of the Jews and the eventual fall of Jerusalem in 70 CE.

At thirty years of age Jesus went to the Judean desert and was baptized by John the Baptist. Thereafter Jesus proclaimed the kingdom of God. Some followed him as his disciples; others, like the Pharisees and other religious leaders, opposed him because of his supposed violations of the Law of Moses. Jesus shared the Pharisees' concern for the Law, and there were many Pharisees who were sympathetic to his message (see Lk 13:31). Jesus' harshest words were for "pharisaism," excessive interpretation of the letter of the Law rather than its spirit. Sometimes, we ourselves are pharisaic in our religious observance while neglecting justice and mercy. We can also be like the Sadducees, so concerned with stability that we are overly cautious and suspicious of any development of religious thought or belief.

Through Jesus' teaching, preaching, and healing, he proclaimed a message of deliverance from everything that kept people from being fully free and fully alive. For those who responded with a sincere desire to hear and obey the good news that Jesus proclaimed, God's reign was at hand. When a scribe asked Jesus what he must do to fulfill God's law, Jesus summed up the Law with two basic commands.

"You shall love the Lord your God with all your heart, and with all your soul, and with all your mind, and with all your strength," and, "You shall love your neighbor as yourself" (Mk 12:30–31; see Deut 6:4–5; Lev 19:18).

Jesus' message and his miracles drew people to the loving embrace of God. When Jesus' disciples observed the intimate way he prayed to the one he called "Father" (Greek, *Pater*; Hebrew, *Ab*; Aramaic, *Abba*, Mk 14:36), they asked him to teach them how to pray (Lk 11:1). He taught them simplicity in prayer by seeking God's will, recognizing

God's providence, asking for forgiveness, and persevering in times of trial (Mt 6:9–13; Lk 11:1–4).

In Jesus' time there was neither king nor kingdom, yet all awaited the time when God's reign would extend over the entire universe. Jesus taught his followers to pray for the coming of God's reign, and he told many parables about its arrival, mysterious, like a tiny mustard seed that grew to become a large tree, or like yeast, a small hidden force that became mighty in time (Mt 13:31–33). Jesus compared the kingdom to seed scattered and sown in God's field. Though most was wasted, some of the seed grew and yielded an incredible harvest (Mk 4:3–8). Jesus said that if we seek God's kingdom before all else, we will be given all that we need (Mt 6:33). In the parable of the "pearl of great price," a merchant sold everything he had in order to obtain this one treasure (13:45–46). These parables challenge us today to examine how highly we rate God's kingdom. Are we willing to put it before all else?

Although Jesus never sought political ambition, his miracles and proclamations aroused a messianic enthusiasm among the people. Many thought he had come to throw off Roman oppression, restore Israel to its former glory, and revive true worship in the Temple. Jesus was outraged by the moneychangers, the buyers and sellers in the Temple who made his Father's "house of prayer" (Mk 11:17) a marketplace. Jesus was accused of blasphemy by the religious authorities who were indignant by his pronouncement that if the Temple were destroyed he would rebuild it in three days (14:58, speaking of his bodily resurrection). Fearing that there would be a political uprising, they looked for a way to kill him. Judas, one of the Twelve Apostles, agreed to betray him.

On the night before he died, Jesus took the ordinary bread and wine of the Passover meal and gave it new meaning. Jesus was God's New Covenant, sealed not by the blood of sacrificial animals but by his own body and blood, the "Lamb of God who takes away the sin of the world" (Jn 1:29). Jesus was arrested and was tried before Pontius Pilate, the Roman governor of Judea (26–36 CE). Pilate judged him to be an agitator who disturbed the Roman peace by his claim to be king of the Jews. Jesus was condemned to death and executed on a cross as a common criminal. When his disciples discovered the empty tomb three days later, the historical Jesus gave way to the Christ of faith.

Christ of Faith

After Jesus' resurrection and glorification, all the limitations he experienced in his human form were removed. We no longer speak of him only as Jesus of Nazareth or Jesus the Galilean. We don't need to pray to him in a particular language. The risen Christ transcends every human difference and each individual can relate to him on a personal basis. Jesus Christ is Lord of all peoples for all time.

The Greek word *Christos* became such a common title for Jesus that it was mistaken as his proper name. "Christ" is not a last name.[3] Jesus was not the son of Mr. and Mrs. Christ. Christ is a title that translates the Hebrew word *Mashiah*, the "anointed one." At the time of Jesus, many Jews looked to the coming of the Messiah, the "day of the Lord" (Joel 1:15), as God's final act in the deliverance and redemption of Israel. Some people hoped in the restoration of a politically independent Judah with a member of the family of David as king. Others looked for a priestly figure, "the Messiah of Aaron." Still others looked for a prophetic leader like Moses (see Deut 18:15). The church sees Jesus fulfilling all these roles as king, priest, and prophet.

The most frequent way Jesus spoke of himself in his earthly ministry was as the "Son of Man," used in the Book of Daniel to designate a human being (7:13; Aramaic, *bar nasa*). The early church understood that Jesus, the "Son of Man," would return in glory at the end of time to receive an "everlasting dominion that shall not pass away" and a kingship "that shall never be destroyed" (7:14).

The risen Christ continues to be present in word and sacrament to heal and give life and grace to the church. God's reign still awaits fulfillment at the end of time, when Christ will return in glory and hand over the kingdom to his Father. At the same time, God's reign is already present "on earth as it is in heaven" (Mt 6:10) when the sick and the poor are cared for and when evil is expelled from our lives and from our world.

Why were the Gospels written?

As the church reflected on the meaning of the risen Christ in its midst, individuals began writing the Gospels. When the apostolic age came to an end with the death of the principle witnesses of Jesus, it was vital for the church to hand on the message to future generations. The Gospels were not historical accounts or biographies of Jesus' life as we might write today. The authors of the Gospels were more interested in conveying Jesus' message, as *Dei Verbum* states:

> The sacred authors wrote the four Gospels, selecting some things from the many which had been handed on by word of mouth or in writing, reducing some of them to a synthesis, explaining some things in view of the situation of their churches and preserving the form of proclamation but always in such fashion that they told us the honest truth about Jesus (DV 19).

Why are there four Gospels?

The Gospels of Matthew, Mark, and Luke are called "synoptic" ("to see with one eye") because they tell a similar story and contain common material. Although the Gospel of John shares some similar material, his portrait of Jesus is quite distinctive. Someone once asked, "Then does John see with two eyes instead of one?" That is not far from the truth. John does see things differently.

In composing the Synoptics, each Gospel writer had sources for the material used. It is believed that Mark's Gospel was the first one written and that both Matthew and Luke used Mark as a major source for their writing. In addition, both Matthew and Luke relied on a lost source that scholars call "Q" from the German word *quelle* or "source." This was probably a collection of sayings of Jesus that was circulated in the early church. Matthew and Luke also had independent material not available to one another. We can diagram this process thus:

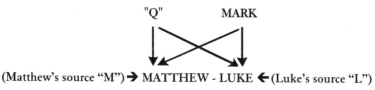

"Q"   MARK

(Matthew's source "M") ➜ MATTHEW - LUKE ⬅ (Luke's source "L")

Each Gospel captures a unique view of Jesus shaped by the perspective of the evangelist and his community. We cannot homogenize the Gospels but must allow each one to be what it is. Just as different artists portray a subject in diverse ways, each portrait of Jesus in the Gospels is unique. By laying parallel passages from the synoptic Gospels in columns we can see how each author told the story of Jesus in a particular way. Many of these features run throughout each Gospel, and once they are grasped, the characteristics of each author can be recognized. Can you find similarities and differences in each account of Jesus' healing in Capernaum?

Mark 1:29–34	*Matthew 8:14–17*	*Luke 4:38–41*
29 As soon as they left the synagogue, they entered the house of Simon and Andrew, with James and John. 30 Now Simon's mother-in-law was in bed with a fever, and they told him about her at once. 31 He came and took her by the hand and lifted her up. Then the fever left her, and she began to serve them. 32 That evening, at sundown, they brought to him all who were sick or possessed with demons. 33 And the whole city was gathered around the door. 34 And he cured many who were sick with various diseases, and cast out many demons; and he would not permit the demons to speak, because they knew him.	14 When Jesus entered Peter's house, he saw his mother-in-law lying in bed with a fever; 15 he touched her hand, and the fever left her, and she got up and began to serve him. 16 That evening they brought to him many who were possessed with demons; and he cast out the spirits with a word, and cured all who were sick. 17 This was to fulfill what had been spoken through the prophet Isaiah, "He took our infirmities and bore our diseases."	38 After leaving the synagogue he entered Simon's house. Now Simon's mother-in-law was suffering from a high fever, and they asked him about her. 39 Then he stood over her and rebuked the fever, and it left her. Immediately she got up and began to serve them. 40 As the sun was setting, all those who had any who were sick with various kinds of diseases brought them to him; and he laid his hands on each of them and cured them. 41 Demons also came out of many, shouting, "You are the Son of God!" But he rebuked them and would not allow them to speak, because they knew that he was the Messiah.

We cannot be sure that the name of the apostle attached to each Gospel (Matthew or John) or an authoritative figure in the community (Mark or Luke) was actually the person who wrote it.

Nevertheless, the church teaches that the Gospels are of apostolic origin, written under the inspiration of the Holy Spirit, and that they faithfully hand on those things that are necessary for our eternal salvation.

Matthew

Matthew's Gospel is placed first in the Bible, not because it is the oldest but because it was used for centuries to catechize Christians. Until Vatican II reforms, it was the principle Gospel read in the liturgy from Sunday to Sunday. Matthew probably wrote his Gospel in Antioch in Syria, sometime between 80–90 CE, to Jewish Christians, as demonstrated by his frequent citations from the Old Testament. After the destruction of the Temple in 70 CE, Jewish converts to Christianity felt cut off from their traditions. Matthew showed them that Jesus was the promised "Messiah, the son of David, the son of Abraham" (1:1). Jesus is "Emmanuel," which means "God is with us" (1:23), the savior through whom salvation would be realized (see Ex 3:12a, "I will be with you"). Central to Matthew's Gospel are five discourses or sermons of Jesus, the most notable being the Sermon on the Mount (5–7). Matthew portrayed Jesus as the new Moses, the teacher of all nations who came to fulfill the Law and give it new meaning. God's blessings and judgment would be on those who did or did not recognize the suffering Christ in the poor and oppressed (25:31–40). Jesus' disciples must be as committed to bringing about the kingdom of God as he was, even at the cost of suffering and death.

Mark

Mark wrote the earliest Gospel, perhaps from Rome, sometime between 66–70 CE, around the time of the destruction of Jerusalem and the Temple. Some scholars suggest that Mark's community was being persecuted for their beliefs during the reign of the emperor Nero in Rome (54–68 CE) where Peter and Paul had already lost their lives as martyrs. Mark wrote his Gospel for gentile Christians who were unfamiliar with Jewish customs. The questions facing these Christians were: What kind of leadership did Jesus model, and why were they being asked to suffer and die for their faith?

At the center of Mark's Gospel, Jesus asked his followers, "Who do you say that I am?" (8:29). Jesus imposed silence on those who misunderstood him as some messianic wonder worker or military hero who would conquer the enemy. If Jesus' disciples wanted to follow him, they must "deny themselves and take up their cross" (8:34) as he did. Mark saw Jesus as the "Son of Man" and as the "suffering servant" of God.[4] Since everyone knew what it meant to experience pain and suffering, the cross became the universal symbol that bound the suffering church together. At the end of Mark's Gospel, it was a gentile Roman soldier at the foot of the cross who proclaimed, "Truly this man was God's Son!" (15:39). Anyone, even a nonbeliever, could see Jesus' true identity.

Luke

Luke wrote two volumes: the Gospel of Luke and the Acts of the Apostles. He wrote either from Antioch (Syria) or Asia Minor (modern Turkey) for Greek-speaking gentiles after the persecution of Nero but while hostilities were still prevalent, probably around 85 CE. According to popular tradition, Luke was an artist. While this cannot be proved, most artists rely on Luke's portrait of Mary in his Gospel for their inspiration of such paintings as the annunciation, the visitation, the birth of Jesus, the presentation and finding in the Temple. Another tradition says that Luke may have been a physician. Paul sent greetings from "Luke, the beloved physician" (Col 4:14). Certainly Luke portrayed a compassionate, healing Jesus whose mission was to liberate people from sickness and oppression. The poor, the outcasts, and women have a special place in Luke's Gospel. Luke told the story of Jesus' humble birth, and he alone recorded Mary's beautiful "magnificat," a hymn of the poor and lowly who were despised by the world but blessed by God (Lk 1:46–55). Only Luke told the parables of God's mercy—the lost coin, the lost sheep, and the prodigal son who "was lost and has been found" (15:32). Only Luke had the merciful Jesus forgiving his enemies from the cross (23:34) and offering salvation to a repentant criminal who was crucified alongside him (23:43).

John

John may have written his Gospel from Ephesus toward the end of the first century. He wrote to a maturing community whose theology was growing and developing. John was not as concerned about the stories of Jesus narrated in the synoptic Gospels but with the meaning behind those stories. John included no infancy narrative as in Matthew and Luke; he began his Gospel with Jesus, the eternal Word made flesh (1:14). John displayed artistic genius in presenting Jesus' words in long poetic discourses. His Jesus was not the suffering servant of the Synoptics but the exalted Son of God and the divine Word of God who offered eternal life to his followers. Throughout John's Gospel, Jesus identified himself as "I AM," the name of God given to Moses at the burning bush (Ex 3:14). "I am the living water" (see Jn 4:10) that quenches thirst. "I am the bread of life" (6:35) that provides daily nourishment. "I am the light of the world" (8:12) that drives out darkness. "I am the vine"—the source of life (15:5). "I am the good shepherd" (10:11), and the guide to eternal life—"I am the resurrection and the life" (11:25).

John did not record Jesus' words of institution at the Last Supper. Instead, he showed Jesus washing the feet of the disciples and telling them, "You also should do as I have done" (13:15). During Lent, the church reads three stories from John's Gospel in preparation for the initiation of new members into the Christian community at Easter. These "scrutiny" stories are: the woman at the well (Jn 4), the man born blind (Jn 9), and the raising of Lazarus (Jn 11). It is a time of conversion for those who are preparing for baptism and also for ourselves. As in the synoptic Gospels, John selected those things necessary to bring people to faith in Jesus Christ. For John, Jesus' mighty deeds were "signs" that pointed to Jesus' true identity as God's Son:

> Now Jesus did many other signs in the presence of his disciples, which are not written in this book. But these are written so that you may come to believe that Jesus is the Messiah, the Son of God, and that through believing you may have life in his name (20:30–31).

Other New Testament Writings

The Acts of the Apostles

Luke's Acts of the Apostles is the story of the church's beginnings. It is not a book of history as such but depicts how the Holy Spirit acted through the church in the first century. Luke is often identified as a companion to Paul on his missionary journeys. Although this is not certain, Paul is the major character in the Book of Acts, and the journey is an important theme in both of Luke's books. In his Gospel, Luke recounted Jesus' journey from Galilee to Jerusalem where he suffered and died (9:51—19:28), and in Acts he related Paul's journey from Jerusalem to Rome, fulfilling Christ's mandate to the apostles to preach the Gospel "to the ends of the earth" (Acts 1:8). In Luke's time, the "ends of the earth" was Rome, the capital of the Roman Empire. The Book of Acts ends abruptly with Paul "proclaiming the kingdom of God and teaching about the Lord Jesus Christ with all boldness and without hindrance" (28:31).

Letters

Paul's letters or "epistles" make up a major portion of the New Testament. Paul did not expect his letters to be read privately as we do today. They were written to the churches he helped establish and shape, and they were usually read aloud in community. Paul had almost nothing to say about the life of Christ (the Jesus of history); everything is about the passion, death, and resurrection of Christ (the Christ of faith): "For I decided to know nothing among you except Jesus Christ, and him crucified" (1 Cor 2:2). Born in human likeness, Jesus was "obedient to the point of death—even death on a cross" (Phil 2:8b). For Paul, the church was the "Body of Christ." Though weak and sinful, it was endowed with different gifts of ministry and service "according to the grace given to us" (Rom 12:6a).

One of Paul's gifts was a tangible sense of the Spirit alive in the church, "for the law of the Spirit of life in Christ Jesus has set you free from the law of sin and of death" (Rom 8:2). Paul discovered that law or ritual practice saved no one. He emphasized the attraction of God's saving grace for those who believed in Christ: "They are now justified by his grace as a gift, through the redemption that is in Christ Jesus" (3:24).

Paul wrote to various communities to address practical matters and to answer moral and ethical questions that had arisen: What should Christians do while waiting for Christ's return? What sort of Jewish practices must they follow? Must non-Jews follow them as well? What was the function of law and faith? What were the roles of men and women, of slaves and converts? How was the Eucharist to be celebrated? Paul gave advice, encouragement, and even rebuke when needed to correct misunderstandings of the Christian message. Paul never intended his writings to be systematic presentations of the faith, nor did he imagine them to be sacred writings, but by 90 CE, they were collected and regarded as Scripture. We can sympathize with Peter and others who tried to understand Paul's complicated theology:

> So also our beloved brother Paul wrote to you according to the wisdom given him, speaking of this as he does in all his letters. There are some things in them hard to understand, which the ignorant and unstable twist to their own destruction, as they do the other scriptures (2 Pet 3:15b–16).

Besides the seven letters written by Paul, there were others written in his name and still other letters written in the name of an apostle (Peter, James, or John) or a non-apostle (Jude).[5] Some letters were written to individuals (Timothy, Titus, and Philemon), others to whole communities (Rome, Corinth, Galatia, Ephesus, Philippi, Colossae, and Thessalonica). The first and second letters to Timothy and the letter to Titus are called "pastoral epistles" since they were written to ministers of the church. Seven epistles—James, 1, 2, and 3 John; 1 and 2 Peter; and Jude—are called "Catholic epistles" since (with the exception of 2 and 3 John) they are not addressed to particular churches but to the church as a whole.[6] The Book of Hebrews is of uncertain authorship and is more of a lengthy sermon than a letter.

The Book of Revelation

The final book in the New Testament is the Book of Revelation, written toward the end of the first century. It is the only book in the

New Testament that belongs to the *apocalyptic* style of literature that was popular around 200 years before and after the time of Christ. It was the major worldview of this period, a belief that the human race was so corrupt it could only be transformed by the establishment of God's reign.

The Greek word *apokalupsis* means "unveiling." The writer's purpose was to *unveil* or *reveal* God's plan for the renewal of the world, thus the name "Apocalypse" or "Revelation." John, the author of the Book of Revelation, recounted a series of visions described in highly symbolic language.[7] Since the Roman Empire would have considered the writing subversive, the author used symbols borrowed from the Hebrew Scriptures, especially the books of Exodus, Daniel, Isaiah, Ezekiel, and Zechariah. The Romans were unable to decipher the bizarre imagery, but first-century Christians understood the underlying reality of the ancient symbols. Because we are not familiar with this style of writing today, there is a great possibility of its being misunderstood as a timetable to predict the end of the world. This is a grave injustice because the central message of the book is hope.

John attempted to stir up the faith of those who had grown apathetic. He also bolstered the faith of those who felt helpless to oppose the powerful empire of Rome, which he depicted as a "beast" ("666") that derived its power from the "dragon" or Satan (Rev 13:11,18).[8] John helped the people of God to raise their eyes from the sufferings of the world by showing them that God's kingdom, not Caesar's, was more powerful than any earthly empire. Jesus Christ had already won the victory on the cross of Calvary. He is the "Lord of Lords" who reigns for all time.

Although proclaimed differently in the Book of Revelation, Jesus Christ was the same person found in Matthew, Mark, Luke, and John and the one announced by Peter and Paul. These books portrayed the living Christ who spoke to each new situation the church experienced. The moral and ethical questions of the first century were not those asked in the sixteenth or the twenty-first century. Similarly, people will be asking different questions in the future because they will be struggling with the unique problems of their times. No generation will exhaust the infinite depth found in God's word.

Endnotes

1. Paul's letters to the Thessalonians reveal the development in theology. In the first letter, Paul anticipated Christ's imminent return at the "sound of God's trumpet" (1 Thess 4:16). The second letter, which may have been written by another author, showed people sitting around idle since Christ's coming had been delayed (2 Thess 2:1–2; 3:11).

2. Paul's dual citizenship is seen in his Hebrew name "Saul" and his Greek name "Paul."

3. People in ancient times did not have last names. They went by their father's name or the place where they lived, for example, Simon son of Jonah or Mary of Magdala.

4. There are four servant songs in the Book of Isaiah: Is 42:1–4; 49:1–6; 50:4–11; 52:13—53:12. The servant's identity has been proposed as some historical or future character, servant Israel, or the prophet himself. God's servant finds its fulfillment in the passion of Jesus Christ.

5. Most scholars are in agreement that Paul wrote the letters to the Romans, 1 and 2 Corinthians, Galatians, Philippians, Philemon, and 1 Thessalonians. There is disagreement as to whether Paul wrote Ephesians, Colossians, 1 and 2 Timothy, 2 Thessalonians, and Titus.

6. The Greek word *katholikos* means "universal." It was first applied to the whole, or universal, church by Ignatius of Antioch: "Wherever the bishop is, there his people should be, just as, where Jesus Christ is, there is the catholic church" (letter to Smyrna, circa 110 CE). The Catholic Church includes churches with a common faith, doctrine, worship, and authority living in communion with the Church of Rome.

7. The author never identified himself as the apostle John but as a "fellow servant" and "prophet" (Rev 22:9) of the community.

8. In Hebrew and Greek, letters had mathematical and also symbolic meanings. The most likely candidate for "666" is Nero Caesar (NRWN QSR), the emperor of Rome who personified the vicious persecution of the church. Thus, $N = 50$, $R = 200$, $W = 6$, $N = 50$ and $Q = 100$, $S = 60$, $R = 200$, added up to the total value of 666. The number may also designate supreme imperfection through its triple repetition of 6 (the perfect number 7 minus 1).

6

Sacred Scripture in the Life of the Church

The Liturgy of the Word

From earliest times, Christians assembled on the Sabbath, the day of the Lord's resurrection. Inspired by faith in the risen Christ, they gathered to break bread in his name. They also kept the Jewish synagogue custom of reading portions of the Hebrew Scriptures—the Law and the Prophets—especially those things in the Scriptures that concerned Jesus (Lk 24:27). Today, Jesus Christ continues to speak to the faithful in the Liturgy of the Word at Mass.

Before Vatican II reforms, we were taught that there were three important parts of the Mass: the offertory, consecration, and communion. The Liturgy of the Word was seen as secondary. The Council changed that picture dramatically. The Liturgy of the Word is no longer just a preparation for the Liturgy of the Eucharist. Both are aspects of the same divine mystery as they "form but one single act of worship" (*Sacrosanctum Concilium* 56).[1] In a like manner, *Dei Verbum* states:

> The Church has always venerated the divine Scriptures just as she venerates the body of the Lord, since, especially in the sacred liturgy, she unceasingly receives and offers to the faithful the bread of life from the table both of God's word and of Christ's body (DV 21).

In the renewal of the liturgy there is the realization that the "real presence" contains such richness and depth that there are at least four different ways that Christ is truly present in the eucharistic celebration:

1. Christ is present in the assembly that gathers to celebrate the sacred mysteries.

2. Christ is present in the priest who leads the assembly in worship and acts in the person of Christ.

3. Christ is present in the Eucharist—body and blood, soul and divinity under the appearances of bread and wine.

4. Christ is present in his word: "It is He Himself who speaks when the holy Scriptures are read in the Church" (SC 7).

The Liturgy of the Word is an encounter with the living Christ present among the faithful. When the Scriptures are read with power in the midst of a believing community, the living word of God is heard. Since Vatican II, the church has radically reformed the Liturgy of the Word, restoring the Bible to its central place both in the liturgy and in the lives of Catholics. The council decreed: "The treasures of the Bible are to be opened up more lavishly, so that richer fare may be provided for the faithful at the table of God's word (SC 51).

The Lectionary

The readings for the liturgy are contained in a book called the lectionary. In the Liturgy of the Word the council restored the earliest tradition of three readings: Old Testament, New Testament, and Gospel. Over a period of three years, a major portion of Scripture is read, with the Gospel being central. The Gospel contains some aspect of Christ's teaching or some event in his life that we must try to understand and apply to our own lives.

The Sunday lectionary uses a three-year cycle based on the three synoptic Gospels. Beginning with the First Sunday of Advent in Year One, we read Matthew. Mark is read in Year Two, and in Year Three we read Luke. Since John's Gospel focuses on the life of the risen Lord, it is featured primarily during the major seasons of Lent and

Easter and Advent and Christmas. John's Gospel also highlights key doctrines such as the Eucharist.

In addition to the Gospel reading, each Sunday has two other readings. The first is usually taken from the Old Testament and was selected in the light of the theme of the Gospel that is read on that Sunday. The second reading is taken from the letters of Paul or one of the other writings of the New Testament and is read semi-continuously. Although the second reading is not always closely connected with the first reading and the Gospel, it provides theological insight and wisdom. Over the course of the three-year cycle we have at least a taste of each of the books of the New Testament. The Second Vatican Council teaches:

> Recalling thus the mysteries of redemption, the Church opens to the faithful the riches of her Lord's powers and merits, so that these are in some way made present for all time, and the faithful are enabled to lay hold upon them and become filled with saving grace (SC 102).

The Liturgical Year

The liturgical year unfolds in light of the paschal mystery, the dying and rising of Jesus Christ. The renewal of the liturgy has as its stated goal the "fully conscious, and active participation in liturgical celebrations" (SC 14). The liturgies we celebrate are not reenactments of historical dramas of the past that we watch passively but an encounter and response to God's saving presence now. Through the liturgy "the work of our redemption is accomplished" (2).[2]

The liturgy enables us to travel from our past-present-future orientation and enter God's timeless salvation expressed by two Greek concepts of time: *chronos*, the time we mark by clocks and calendars, and *kairos*, the eternal moment of God's saving work. The wonderful events we read about in the Gospels are happening *now*. During Advent and Christmas we experience the birth and rebirth of the Messiah in our lives *now*. On Good Friday we sing, "Were you there when they crucified my Lord?" and the answer is, "Yes! We are there *now!*" On Easter, we are not merely remembering something that happened two thousand years ago; Christ rises in us *now*. Similarly, on Pentecost the Spirit is given today and every day. Reading Scripture in the context of the liturgical year proclaims this marvelous truth again and again.

God's Word in Our Daily Lives

Dei Verbum affirms that sacred Scripture must nourish all preaching and teaching. Clergy, religious, deacons, and catechists are especially encouraged to learn the "surpassing value of knowing Christ Jesus" (Phil 3:8). Then none will be "an empty preacher of the Word of God outwardly, who is not a listener to it inwardly" (DV 25).[3]

Dei Verbum urges all the Catholic faithful to know Christ by frequent reading of the Scriptures, through liturgical proclamations, catechetical instruction, devotional reading, and Bible study. As followers of Christ, we must know Christ, and to know Christ, we must know the Scriptures. As St. Jerome puts it, "Ignorance of the Scriptures is ignorance of Christ" (DV 25).[4]

The Senses of Scripture

St. Thomas Aquinas, theologian and Doctor of the Church, points out in his *Summa Theologiae* that the Bible is a special kind of book like no other, inasmuch as it has two senses expressed in the very same words:

1. **The literal sense** seeks to uncover the meaning that has been expressed by the inspired human authors following the rules of sound biblical exegesis.[5]

2. **The spiritual sense** seeks the guidance of the Holy Spirit to read the sacred text in light of the paschal mystery of Christ and to experience the new life that flows from it.

The Literal Sense

As we read and reflect on a biblical passage, it is important to place the text in the literary, historical, social, cultural, political, and religious world in which it was written. We need to ask ourselves what the passage meant to the people to whom it was written. We can use the story of Jesus healing the blind man as an example of how to read the Scriptures.

> As [Jesus] and his disciples and a large crowd were leaving Jericho, Bartimaeus son of Timaeus, a blind beggar, was sitting by the roadside. When he heard that it was Jesus of Nazareth, he began to shout out and say, "Jesus, Son of David, have mercy on me!" Many sternly ordered him to be quiet, but he cried out even more loudly, "Son of David, have mercy on me!" Jesus stood still and said, "Call him here." And they called the blind man, saying to him, "Take heart; get up, he is calling you." So throwing off his cloak, he sprang up and came to Jesus. Then Jesus said to him, "What do you want me to do for you?" The blind man said to him, "My teacher, let me see again." Jesus said to him, "Go; your faith has made you well." Immediately he regained his sight and followed him on the way (Mk 10:46–52).

For the literal sense of this short passage, we need to ask, what is the background?[6] We can go to the footnotes or reading guide in our Bibles to find answers.[7] We can also look up information in a Bible commentary, biblical dictionary, or atlas. We learn that Bartimaeus is not a personal name; he is the "son of Timaeus" (Aramaic, *Bar Timai*). Of historical interest we note that Jericho, first mentioned in Joshua's conquest of the land (Josh 2:1), is the site of the oldest city ever discovered, dating back to 10,000 BCE. Along the roads and at the gates of a city, beggars often pleaded for alms. Due to lack of hygiene and medical care, blindness was as common in ancient times as it is in areas of the Third World today.

Then we need to ask, what did the passage mean in its own day? Again, we need to do some reading. We find in the time of Jesus that the poor, the lepers, the lame, and the blind were outcasts of society, but he made them the object of his ministry. Although Mark pictured the apostles as blind to the meaning of Jesus' message, Bartimaeus received his sight and "immediately" (a favorite word of Mark) followed Jesus on "the way." Mark showed Jesus constantly taking his message on the "road" (Greek, *hodos*; Hebrew, *derek*), and we learn that early Christians were simply called followers of "the way."

When we read the sacred text from the literal sense, our reading is primarily for its intellectual value. Though knowledge is important for our understanding, we can't understand God's word only through doctrines and theologies. It is possible to be doctrinally correct and spiritually dead. An accumulation of facts does not necessarily produce persons of faith.

The Spiritual Sense

The spiritual sense builds on the literal sense and is of equal importance. St. Augustine, in his book *De Utilitate Credendi*, differentiated four senses of Scripture: the literal, the allegorical, the moral, and the mystical. We can use the city of Jerusalem as an example of all four senses:

1. **The literal sense** is the meaning expressed directly by the words of the sacred writers; for example, the actual city of Jerusalem in Palestine.

2. **The allegorical sense** is a drawn-out metaphor, a description of one thing under the image of another; for example, the city of Jerusalem as a symbol for the faithful or unfaithful people of God.

3. **The moral sense** is an interpretation of Scripture in a moralistic sense; for example, St. Paul tells the Corinthians not to commit fornication since, just as the Temple in Jerusalem was defiled, they will defile themselves, the living temple of God, in doing so (1 Cor 3:16–17).

4. **The mystical (eschatological) sense** reveals a hidden spiritual meaning of the end-times, the "four last things," namely, death, judgment, heaven, and hell; for example, the church as a sign of the heavenly Jerusalem (Rev 21:1—22:5).

This method of finding four meanings in Scripture prevailed throughout the Middle Ages and is still popular today. In order to arrive at the deeper significance of the text we need God's grace through the Holy Spirit. By asking questions from our personal experience, we find that the biblical story also becomes our story. In the story of Jesus healing the blind man we might ask:

- What is God's word to me today?

- Why do I find it so difficult to obey God's word to love and serve others?

- Am I blind to those around me in need? If so, what will it take to open my eyes?

- How can I apply God's word to my life in ways that build God's kingdom on earth?

The word of God is different than other forms of literature. While other books may inform us, Scripture has the power to form us and even transform us. The Hebrew word *yada* is "to know from the heart." Like Moses, we should radiate God's presence to others because we have first spoken intimately with God (Ex 34:29). To do this we must wrestle with God's word as Jacob contended with the angel (Gen 32:24–31), an experience that left him changed forever. Thereafter Jacob walked with a limp as a sign of his divine encounter. Our experience need not be so drastic, but the Bible should leave its mark on us. The word of God is not only to be studied; it is to be accepted and lived.

Encountering God's word always challenges us to know God's will and follow it more closely. When Jesus told the rich man to give his money to the poor and then come and follow him, the rich man "went away grieving, for he had many possessions" (Mt 19:22). In contrast, Bartimaeus threw aside his cloak, possibly his only earthly possession, and followed Jesus immediately. Christianity is a "way," not just an academic discipline. If we are in search of spiritual growth we need to go beyond information to transformation through prayer.

Prayer and Scripture

Dei Verbum reminds us that prayer should accompany the reading of sacred Scripture, for "'we speak to Him when we pray; we hear Him when we read the divine saying'" (DV 25).[8] Reading the Bible prayerfully develops our relationship with God. We become aware of God's love for us and experience peace and joy. At the same time we sense our own sinfulness and need for healing and reconciliation.

Through God's grace we are able to respond with thanksgiving, faith, and trust.

Not every part of the Bible is helpful for prayer, such as the long genealogical lists and law codes. We might begin with passages that are familiar to us—Abraham's call (Gen 17:1–9); Moses at the burning bush (Ex 3:1–7) or on Mount Sinai (19:16–25); Jesus calming the storm (Mk 4:35–41) or the woman who reached out to be healed by him (5:25–34). The psalms are especially helpful in praying Scripture.

The Psalms — The Prayer Book of the Bible

The Book of Psalms is the prayer book or the songbook of God's people. Jesus, Mary and Joseph used the psalms in their home in Nazareth, and later they became the prayers of the church. The psalms can be our personal prayers too. To pray with the psalms is to discover the full range of human emotions. We can sing out in praise or cry out in pain. We can pray in times of trust and in times of fear, in times of hope and in times of despair.

The Hebrew name of the Book of Psalms is *Sefer Tehillim*, which translates as the "Book of Praises." Yet the psalms of lament comprise the largest collection of prayers in the psalter. How can these complaints be considered words of praise? In the biblical mind, the lament was considered an expression of praise even in moments of suffering. On the cross, Jesus prayed Psalm 22 in agony, yet with confidence in God:

> My God, my God, why have you forsaken me?
>> Why are you so far from helping me, from the words of my groaning?
> O my God, I cry by day, but you do not answer;
>> and by night, but find no rest.
>
> Yet you are holy,
>> enthroned on the praises of Israel (Ps 22:1–3; see Mt 27:46).

A four-step method of praying the psalms can also be a means for praying any Scripture passage:

1. Pause

2. Ponder

3. Personalize

4. Pray

The classical definition of prayer is that of lifting the mind and heart to God so that through the power of the Holy Spirit we can enter into a conversation with God. It may be helpful to find a comfortable position, close your eyes, and become aware of your breathing. Pray, "Come Holy Spirit, fill the hearts of your faithful and enkindle in them the fire of your love." You might repeat a simple phrase (mantra) such as "Jesus is Lord" or the Jesus prayer, "Jesus Christ, Son of God, Savior," or make up your own mantra such as: "Today I will live in the light of God's word." Become aware of God's presence—the Holy Spirit who is praying in you, through you, with you, and for you.

Pause

The Bible gives us words for our prayers, but the basic attitude of prayer is listening. Spend a few minutes quieting yourself, "like a weaned child with its mother" (Ps 131:2). Ask the Spirit for the grace to listen to God's word. Select a psalm for prayer such as Psalm 139:

1 O LORD, you have searched me and known me.
2 You know when I sit down and when I rise up; / you discern my thoughts from far away.
3 You search out my path and my lying down, / and are acquainted with all my ways.
4 Even before a word is on my tongue, / O LORD, you know it completely.
5 You hem me in, behind and before, / and lay your hand upon me.
6 Such knowledge is too wonderful for me; / it is so high that I cannot attain it.

Ponder

Read the psalm, trying to get a sense of the whole. It may be helpful to read the footnotes or a commentary if something seems obscure. Then read the psalm again slowly. This is not a time for information or profound insight but simply for reflecting on God's presence of healing, strength, love, and peace. You may be moved to respond in some way.

Personalize

Now read the psalm once again. This time you may want to put your name in the psalm as you pray. You may also want to make a few notes in a journal. Writing helps you to get in touch with yourself and your relationship with God and others. Perhaps your response will take the form of a meditation, a letter, or even write your own psalm. Be creative. Don't be concerned about following rules or doing it right. It is impossible to do it wrong! Just jot down whatever comes to your mind as you ask yourself:

- What thoughts or emotions did I experience?

- Can I praise God for my joys as well as petition God in my struggles?

- Can I give thanks for God's wondrous love?

- Am I able to connect with others in the world who are mourning, praising, and pleading, like the psalmists, even if that isn't my prayer at the moment?

Pray

Pray the psalm slowly and attentively. Linger on words or phrases that have a special meaning to you. Hold them in your heart and let them speak to you. Listen as the beloved listens to the lover. Speak to God who is dwelling within you and respond with gratitude and love. Ask God to help you to obey the sacred word. Don't be discouraged if you only experience dry and empty feelings. God accepts our inability to pray at times. Remember Paul's words:

The Spirit helps us in our weakness; for we do not know how to pray as we ought, but that very Spirit intercedes with sighs too deep for words. And God, who searches the heart, knows what is the mind of the Spirit, because the Spirit intercedes for the saints according to the will of God (Rom 8:26–27).

Lectio Divina

Lectio Divina (Latin, "divine reading") is another method of praying with Scripture. It, too, involves a slow, contemplative reading as a means of union with God. The Benedictine tradition urges us to listen deeply, to hear "with the ear of our hearts" (Prologue to the Rule of St. Benedict). *Lectio Divina* helps us connect our personal stories with the biblical story—our joys and sorrows, longings and hopes, exiles and homecomings. This is not merely *reading* God's word but seeking to *become one* with it, allowing it to nourish us. The biblical image is to "eat the word," as did the prophet Ezekiel:

Mortal, eat this scroll that I give you and fill your stomach with it. Then I ate it; and in my mouth it was as sweet as honey. He said to me: Mortal, go to the house of Israel and speak my very words to them (Ezek 3:3–4).

When we find that God's word has become part of our very being, we are empowered to speak God's words. The *Lectio Divina* process offers us this kind of nourishment:

- *Lectio:* **Read (Bite):** Read God's word in "bite size" pieces. The monastic tradition says it is better to read one verse from Scripture well than to read whole volumes poorly.

- *Meditatio:* **Meditate (Chew):** Meditate and reflect on God's word, like Mary who asked, "How can this be?" (Lk 1:34) as she "treasured all these words and pondered them in her heart" (2:19).

- *Oratio:* Pray **(Digest):** Respond prayerfully to God with adoration, thanksgiving, petition, intercession, and praise.

- *Contemplatio*: **Contemplate (Nourish):** Enter into silence and rest in God's presence. The psalmist says, "Be still, and know that I am God!" (Ps 46:10). Say with Samuel, "Speak, for your servant is listening" (1 Sam 3:10). Surrender like Mary, "Here am I, the servant of the Lord; let it be with me according to your word" (Lk 1:38).

Just as there is a need to receive spiritual nourishment from Jesus' body and blood in the Eucharist, there is a need to be nourished by God's word in the Scriptures. At the table of the word, the inner attitudes of our hearts and minds are formed so that we can approach the table of the Eucharist properly.

The Ignatian Way of Praying Scripture

St. Ignatius of Loyola, the founder of the Jesuits, offers another way of praying with Scripture. In his *Spiritual Exercises*, a guide for making a retreat and for living our lives, St. Ignatius invites us to put ourselves in the story. He says that we should use all of our senses as we immerse ourselves in the Scripture passage—what we see, hear, touch, and even what we smell and taste:

- What do you see in the biblical scene?—the city, desert, mountains, forests, or the sea?

- What do you hear—the voice of the prophet, of Jesus, of the people?

- What do you touch—the hand of Jesus reaching out to you, your hand reaching to touch the hem of his garment?

- What do you smell—the fragrance of wind and rain, the lilies of the field?

- Can you taste God's presence—the salt and oil, water, bread and wine?

In meditating on the Scriptures this way, become aware of your response—joy, sadness, anger, discomfort—and consider what it might mean for you at this time. An excellent illustration of the power of praying Scripture in the Ignatian way is Luke's story of the "Road to Emmaus."

The Ignatian Way to Emmaus: Luke 24:13–32

As in all methods of praying with Scripture, begin with a prayer for the grace to listen to the Holy Spirit speaking to you. Then read the passage all the way through. If you are doing this exercise in a group, ask one person to read the text out loud. Visualize the setting as vividly as you can. Take a moment to get in touch with all your senses. Insert yourself into the scene, imagining that you are one of the characters in the story. Observe your feelings. What is the climate—not just the weather but also your emotional climate?

- **Read Luke 24:13–14**

  Imagine: Close your eyes and picture yourself as the unnamed disciple in the story walking along the road to your home in Emmaus, a seven-mile journey from Jerusalem. You are walking away from the tragedy you have just witnessed on Calvary. You realize that you are not alone as you travel the road. Walking along with you is your companion whose name is Cleopas. Who might this person represent? What is your relationship with him or her? What are your feelings—sadness, disappointment, or hopelessness?

  Reflect: All of life is a series of Emmaus moments, and we are all pilgrims on a journey. Even though we are traveling with others, no one's spiritual journey is like any other. We are trying to reach the same destination, but sometimes we move forward, and at other times we go backward or even stand still. Like the disciples of Emmaus, we may travel in the wrong direction, away from the sunrise of Easter toward the nightfall of Emmaus.

- **Read verses 15–16**

  Imagine: Envision a stranger appearing and walking alongside you. What keeps you from recognizing Jesus? Does it seem at times that he is absent and silent in your life? Do you feel alone in your pain and deserted in your hour of need? At such moments, do you feel that it is more like Good Friday than Easter Sunday?

Reflect: At those times when we do not feel Jesus' presence, he does not say, "Open your eyes! Don't you see me? I am right here with you!" Instead, he enters into a conversation with us so we can have communion with him. Jesus told his disciples, "Where two or three are gathered in my name, I am there among them" (Mt 18:20).

• **Read verses 17–21**

Imagine: Picture Jesus walking beside you. Hear him ask, "What are you talking about as you walk along?" Share with him your problems, disappointments, or loss of hope. It may be a marriage or a job failure, the diagnosis of a doctor, or simply an argument with a friend. Be honest in telling him whatever is on your mind. How does Jesus respond to your concerns?

Reflect: The disciples of Emmaus were completely shattered by the recent events in Jerusalem. They longed for a savior, and now they utter the sad words, "We hoped that he was the one to set us free." They forgot the words Jesus spoke to his disciples: "If you continue in my word, you are truly my disciples; and you will know the truth, and the truth will make you free" (Jn 8:31–32). Jesus beckons in our darkness and shows us the way to go: "I am the light of the world. Whoever follows me will never walk in darkness but will have the light of life" (8:12).

• **Read verses 22–24**

Imagine: Go back in your imagination to Jerusalem. It is Easter morning as you walk to the tomb. Who else goes with you? What are your feelings when you find that it is empty? Are you frightened or bewildered? How do you respond when you see no evidence of answered prayer and others scoff at your beliefs? Are there lessons to learn in times of darkness and disbelief?

Reflect: Do you feel at times like Jesus' disciples, lost on a dark road, trying to find your way back home? Then Jesus comes walking toward you. Listen to his voice as he calms your fears and anxieties, "Take heart, it is I; do not be afraid" (Mt 14:27). Ask Jesus to give you the determination to keep walking when the path is rough and for strength to get up whenever you stumble and fall.

• **Read verses 25–27**

Imagine: Picture Jesus opening the Scriptures and explaining them to you. Is Jesus unlocking your heart or is the Bible a closed book for you? Do you find the mystery of suffering a sign of God's punishment and rejection? Are you asking, "Why should it be God's will for anyone to suffer? Is this the way God shows love for me?" Listen to Jesus' words: "If any want to become my followers, let them deny themselves and take up their cross and follow me. For those who want to save their life will lose it, and those who lose their life for my sake, and for the sake of the gospel, will save it" (Mk 8:34b–35).

Reflect: In moments of tragedy and loss we are not satisfied with simple answers. We find ourselves up against the mystery of God, who says, "For my thoughts are not your thoughts, nor are your ways my ways" (Is 55:8). At such times we can only hope and believe that God's ways are good and loving. If it was necessary that Jesus suffer so as to enter glory, might it not be necessary for us to walk a similar path?

• **Read verses 28–29**

Imagine: Slowly, you begin to feel a spark of hope, but you notice that the light in the sky is gradually fading. If Jesus left now, you would be completely in the dark. What emotions do you feel—fear, anxiety, distress, hope? Hear yourself pleading with Jesus, "Stay with me! Abide with me!"

Reflect: Jesus wants to abide with us. He wants us to meet him in prayer, word, and sacrament. He said, "I am the bread of life. Whoever comes to me will never be hungry, and whoever believes in me will never be thirsty" (Jn 6:35). He waits for our invitation: "Listen! I am standing at the door, knocking; if you hear my voice and open the door, I will come in to you and eat with you, and you with me" (Rev 3:20).

- **Read verses 30–32**

  Imagine: Hear yourself inviting Jesus to enter your home. How does Jesus respond to your invitation? How does this make you feel? Excited? Apprehensive? Embarrassed? What is your spiritual home like? Is it warm and hospitable or dark and uninviting? Are there rooms or closets that are closed? Are you ashamed to open them to God? Do you feel empty and dissatisfied?

  Reflect: The word of God is not just printing on a piece of paper; it is God made flesh (Jn 1:14). When we come to know Jesus in the word, then we can recognize him in the breaking of the bread. We no longer need Jesus' physical presence. Through the Holy Spirit he eternally abides in the church, in his sacred word, and in his eucharistic presence. He also abides in our hearts and in our homes.

- **Read verses 33–35**

  Imagine: See yourself heading back to Jerusalem to share the good news with the other disciples. Does the road seem different now? As you enter the house where Jesus' disciples are gathered, how do they greet you? Feel the joy as you and your companion proclaim: "Were not our hearts burning within us while he was talking to us on the road, while he was opening the scriptures to us?" (Lk 24:32).

  Reflect: Remain in silence for some period. When you feel ready, open your eyes and come back to the present world. The process is not over once we close the Bible; there is still another step we need to take. We need to put our reflection into action. At the last judgment there will be a final test. Jesus won't ask us how many times we read the Bible or how many verses we memorized. He will ask how well we understood his message. Fortunately he not only gives us the questions, he gives the answers too:

Then the righteous will answer him, "Lord, when was it that we saw you hungry and gave you food, or thirsty and gave you something to drink?

And when was it that we saw you a stranger and welcomed you, or naked and gave you clothing? And when was it that we saw you sick or in prison and visited you?" And the king will answer them, "Truly I tell you, just as you did it to one of the least of these who are members of my family, you did it to me" (Mt 25:37–40).

Conclusion

Living the good news is a challenge for every believer, as is sharing it. Paul said to "proclaim the message; be persistent whether the time is favorable or unfavorable; convince, rebuke, and encourage, with the utmost patience in teaching" (2 Tim 4:2). Peter wrote, "Always be ready to make your defense to anyone who demands from you an accounting for the hope that is in you; yet do it with gentleness and reverence" (1 Pet 3:15b–16a). The Gospel is not only to be discussed or argued; the good news of Jesus Christ is to be lived through word and action. For St. Francis, preaching the Gospel was a witness of life: "Preach Christ always; if necessary, use words."

Mary is the biblical model of one who heard the word of God and obeyed it with humility and faith (Lk 11:28). Despite apprehension, she accepted God's word and gave birth to Jesus. Like Mary, the "God bearer" (Greek, *Theotokos*), our vocation is to bear Christ to a world of suffering and sin. Each of us must write a "fifth Gospel" by the way that we live our lives. We must be careful, for it may be the only Gospel that some people will ever read.

The document on Divine Revelation ends with an expression of hope:

In this way, therefore, through the reading and study of the sacred books "the word of God may spread rapidly and be glorified" (2 Thess 3:1) and the treasure of revelation, entrusted to the Church, may more and more fill the hearts of men. Just as the life of the Church is strengthened through more frequent celebration of the Eucharistic mystery, similar[ly] we may hope for a new stimulus for the life of the Spirit from a growing reverence for the word of God, which "lasts forever" (Is. 40:8; see 1 Peter 1:23–25), (DV 26).

Endnotes

1. The translation of the *Constitution on the Sacred Liturgy, Sacrosanctum Concilium* (SC), used in this book is from the Vatican website. Go to www.vatican.va/archive/hist_councils /ii_vatican_council/ and clicking on the document name.

2. This excerpt from SC 2 contains note #1 as follows: 2. RM, prayer over the gifts, Holy Thursday and 2d Sunday in Ordinary Time.

3. This excerpt from DV 25 contains note #4 as follows: 4. St. Augustine Sermons, 179,1: PL 38,966.

4. This excerpt from DV 25 contains note #5 as follows: 5. St. Jerome, Commentary on Isaiah, Prol.: PL 24,17. cf. Benedict XV, encyclical "Spiritus Paraclitus:" EB 475–480; Pius XII, encyclical "Divino Afflante Spiritu:" EB 544.

5. Exegesis (to draw out the meaning) is the critical analysis, explanation, and interpretation of a word or passage in the Bible. Its opposite is eisegesis, reading our own bias or assumptions into a text.

6. A short passage from a written work that can stand alone is called a *pericope* (Greek, literally to "cut around").

7. The Catholic Study Bible is recommended for its extensive notes and reading guide. See the bibliography at the end of this book.

8. This excerpt from DV 25 contains note #6 as follows: 6. St. Ambrose, On the Duties of Ministers I, 20,88: PL 16,50.

Bibliography:
Basic Tools for Bible Study

D*ei Verbum* urges easy access to the sacred Scriptures for all the Christian faithful. Catholic scholars and those who work in the field of sacred theology are encouraged to combine their efforts under the guidance of the church. Using appropriate techniques they should examine and explain the sacred texts in such a way that they nourish the people of God, "to enlighten their minds, strengthen their wills, and set men's hearts on fire with the love of God" (DV 23).[1] With the approval and active support of the shepherds of the church, correct translations of Scripture, commentaries, references, and other aids are to be made available to everyone everywhere. Here are some tools Catholics need in their study of the Bible.

Modern Versions of the Bible

Bible in Today's English (Good News Bible). New York: American Bible Society, 1992. This Bible is accurate and faithful to the meaning found in the original Greek and Hebrew texts. It uses the principle of dynamic equivalence, in which the translation expresses the meaning of the original text by using its everyday English equivalent so that everyone can appreciate it regardless of age or background.

The current edition uses inclusive language but lacks extensive footnotes.

New American Bible. New York: Oxford University Press, 1990. The NAB is based on the 1970 translation from the original languages and includes the revised New Testament. This version, used in the lectionary, reflects gender inclusivity and improved language for public proclamation. The NAB *Catholic Study Bible* contains excellent notes, reference articles, and a reading guide for each book of the Bible.

New Jerusalem Bible. New York: Doubleday Books, a division of Random House, Inc., 1985. The NJB was translated from the 1966 French edition. The revised version includes improved text and footnotes offering help with difficult passages, background information, and inclusive language.

New Revised Standard Version. New York: Division of Christian Education of the National Council of the Churches of Christ in the United States of America, 1989. The NRSV is based on the 1955 translation, the Revised Standard Version (a further revision of the King James Version of 1611). It contains the Catholic and Orthodox Christian deuterocanonical books. It is accurate and elegant in expression and has greater gender inclusivity. It is the text used in the English edition of the *Catechism of the Catholic Church.*

The Living Bible and similar paraphrased versions are not recommended for study purposes. These are not translations but a rewording or amplification of the original texts in an attempt to clarify the written word. It is easy to see how the particular bias of these interpreters can influence the meaning of the text.

Other Useful Reference Tools

Dei Verbum: Dogmatic Constitution on Divine Revelation.
  In *Vatican Council II: The Conciliar and Post Conciliar Documents,* edited by Austin Flannery. Northport, N.Y.: Costello Publishing, Co. Inc., 1996.

Documents of the Pontifical Biblical Commission

Instruction on the Historical Truth of the Gospels. (April 21, 1964). [Acta Apostolicae Sedis 56 (1964) 712–718].

The Interpretation of the Bible in the Church. (April 15, 1993). [*Libreria Editrice Vaticana* Vatican City, 1993].

The Jewish People and their Sacred Scriptures in the Christian Bible. (May 24, 2001). [*Libreria Editrice Vaticana*, Vatican City 2001].

Introductions to the Scriptures

Boadt, Lawrence. *Reading the Old Testament: An Introduction.* Mahwah, N.J.: Paulist Press, 1984.

Brown, Raymond E. *An Introduction to the New Testament.* New York: Doubleday, 1996.

Bible Commentaries

Brown, Raymond E., Joseph A. Fitzmyer, and Roland E. Murphy, eds. *The New Jerome Biblical Commentary*, Englewood Cliffs, N.J.: Prentice-Hall, Inc., 1990.

Farmer, William R., ed. *The International Bible Commentary.* Collegeville, Minn.: The Liturgical Press, 1998.

Karris, Robert J., ed. *Collegeville Bible Commentary.* Collegeville, Minn.: The Liturgical Press, 1983. Old and New Testament series is available either as individual booklets or one entire commentary and includes many different authors.

Mays, James L., ed. *Harper Collins Bible Commentary.* San Francisco: Harper San Francisco, 2000.

Bible Dictionaries

Achtemeier, Paul J., ed. *Harper Collins Bible Dictionary.* San Francisco: Harper San Francisco, 1996.

Metzger, Bruce M., and Michael D. Coogan, eds. *The Oxford Companion to the Bible.* New York: Oxford University Press, 1993.

Stuhlmueller, Carroll, ed. *The Collegeville Pastoral Dictionary of Biblical Theology.* Collegeville, Minn.: The Liturgical Press, 1996.

Periodicals

Bosnick, Anthony, ed. *Share the Word*. Washington, D.C.: Paulist National Catholic Evangelization Association. Published seven times a year. Contains commentaries on the Sunday Mass readings, reflections on the weekday Mass readings, and articles by leading experts.

Martin, George, ed. *God's Word Today*. Boulder, Co.: University of St. Thomas. A daily reading guide published monthly. A Scripture reading assignment for each day of the month, together with a practical commentary and pointers for personal reflection and insightful articles. Ideal for individual or group study of the Bible.

Senior, Donald, ed. *The Bible Today*. Collegeville, Minn.: The Liturgical Press. Published six times a year in understandable and instructive language.

Shanks, Hershel, ed. *Biblical Archaeology Review*. Washington, D.C.: Biblical Archaeology Society. Published bimonthly. The Biblical Archaeology Society educates the public about archaeology and the Bible through the latest that scholarship has to offer in an accessible manner. Visit www.biblicalarchaeology.org.

Resources from Kay Murdy

From Pharaoh to the Father: A Journey toward Freedom through the Lord's Prayer. San Jose, Calif.: Resource Publications, Inc., 2000.

Ninety Days: Daily Reflections for Lent and Easter. San Jose, Calif.: Resource Publications, Inc., 1995.

Season of Emmanuel: Daily Reflections for Advent, Christmas and Epiphany. San Jose, Calif.: Resource Publications, Inc., 1996.

Online Resources

- **Resource Publications, Inc.:** Resources for ministry, worship, and education. http://www.rpinet.com.

- **Daily Word of Life, Kay Murdy, MA:** Commentaries on the weekday and Sunday Scripture readings of the liturgy; home Bible study; prayer, news, and events of interest to Catholics. http://www.daily-word-of-life.com.

- **Felix Just, SJ, PhD.**: Director, Center for Religion and Spirituality, Loyola Marymount University, Los Angeles. Contains materials related to academic biblical studies useful for scholars, teachers, students, and many others. http://bellarmine.lmu.edu/~fjust.

- **New American Bible:** Full text of the Bible, in canonical order; from the official website of the United States Council of Catholic Bishops. http://www.nccbuscc.org/nab/bible/index.htm.

- **The five Gospels parallels:** Allows side-by-side views of Matthew, Mark, Luke, and John, and the non-canonical Gospel of Thomas http://www.utoronto.ca/religion/synopsis/.

- **Vatican Council II documents.:** http://www.vatican.va/archive/hist_councils/ii_vatican_council. Click on document name.

Endnote

1. This excerpt from DV 23 contains note #1 as follows: 1. cf. Pius XII, encyclical "Divino Afflante Spiritu:" EB 551, 553, 567. Pontifical Biblical Commission, Instruction on Proper Teaching of Sacred Scripture in Seminaries and Religious Colleges, May 13, 1950: A.A.S. 42 (1950) pp. 495–505.